Dedication

This book is dedicated to our Lord and Savior,
Jesus Christ.

Acknowledgments

My deepest appreciation and love to my
wife Andrea, for her understanding and
support, and for our girls, Christal, Summer
and Lauren for their spiritual zeal,
encouragement and constant joy.

HOW ON EARTH CAN WE PLEASE GOD?

40 Days of Prayer

SEEKING GOD'S FACE

© 2009 by Johnson Chiu

International Standard Book Number 978-0-9819878-0-4

Cover design and interior design by Daniel Chou

Scripture quotations are from:
New International Version Bible (NIV) (c) 1985
The Zondervan Corporation

Printed in the United States of America

For information:
Johnson Chiu
faithwalk40@yahoo.com

HOW ON EARTH CAN WE PLEASE GOD?

40 Days of Prayer

SEEKING GOD'S FACE

40 Days of Prayer

SEEKING GOD'S FACE

Table of Contents

Introduction from *Pastor Johnson Chiu*

During the next 40 days, we will embark on a spiritual journey together. 40 Days of Prayer is designed to take us from the beginning steps of prayer to being believers devoted to prayer. We will discover the incredible richness available to us when we pray. God longs to hear and answer our prayers.

A key for our study is "praying together." Take advantage of a group setting; whether it is during Sunday worship, our Wednesday corporate prayer gatherings, in a small group, around the kitchen table or at the lunch room at work. Individual prayer is needed as well. We're simply enhancing our spiritual lives by praying together. Think of working out at the gym. Why do most people work out at the gym? It is not just for the fancy equipment. The number one reason is motivation. Most of us need all the motivation and encouragement we can get. When we pray together we are stronger together.

The question we will answer in the course of this devotional is "How on earth can we please God?" It's a daunting task if we were to strike out on our own. By following God and listening to what pleases Him, it is a delight. In essence this devotional brings us back to the place where we allow God to be God. He gets to lead in our lives. We will discover that prayer is for everyone. This devotional is set up in six distinct sections. Days 1-7 deal with "God's call for us to pray." We will see how important it is for us to go to God. Days 8-14 centers on "Praying for God's Pleasure." This section develops our relationship with God. Days 15-21 focus on "Pray for Outreach." Here we see how vital prayer is to evangelism. Days 22-28 looks at "Pray for Mutual Encouragement." God instructs us on the workings of the Holy Spirit among believers. Days 29-35 pinpoints "Pray for Our Growth." We will see that life lived in God accelerates our spiritual lives. We conclude with Days 36-40, "Pray for Other Believers." Here we look at common prayer needs and how we can pray for others.

This book was designed specifically for you. There are hundreds of Bible verses throughout the book. As you read each day's devotion, take note of the verses and how they relate to you. God promises His Word will be effective. Concentrate on the Bible verses as you come across them. His Word is active and will speak to you if you are sensitive to His Word. Read each day with a prayerful heart.

This book was meant as a manual for you to put into practice. You will see a summary section at the back of each day's devotion. Don't skip this section. Spend time in responding to what God is saying to you. Only what is put into practice counts. Give yourself a few moments after each day's reading to reflect and pray! Ask God to give you spiritual understanding and personal steps of application.

Years ago, God brought me to the place of confessing my own prayerlessness. I devoted myself to God to pray at least an hour a day in seeking the Lord. I've enjoyed wonderful times of communion as I have kept my appointment with God. As a result of spiritual growth and direction from God, we grew as a people, planted a church, saw the hand of God work in transforming lives. All of these things and more were born out of prayer.

We are on the cusp of revival, whether individual or corporate. Revival is a spiritual venture. It cannot be mustered up by our own hands. It will not come until God is exalted among His people. We are at such a time in history where the winds of the Spirit will come in power, bringing refreshment and vitality to the nation.

The beginning of God's revival has already begun. A look at the spiritual landscape across our country reveals pockets of believers gathering together and God's power transforming entire towns, cities and churches. People devoting themselves to the Lord and pouring out their lives in prayer and praise is more common than ever.

It is my prayer that we continue in what God has already begun across our great land. 40 Days of Prayer can be the greatest adventure you have ever experienced.

God's Call to Pray

Day 1

DON'T JUST DO SOMETHING — PRAY!

> *Call to me and I will answer you and tell you great and unsearchable things you do not know.*
> (Jeremiah 33:3)

Go to God first.

God has so much for us if only we would pray to Him! He delights when we go to Him, call out to Him and seek Him for everything — in good times, bad times and ordinary times. During the next 40 days, we are going to develop a lifestyle of seeking God. We want tos know what God has in store for us each day and the only way we are going to know is by going to God.

You have in your hands the 40 Days of Prayer entitled, "How on earth can we please God?" To get the most out of it, I encourage you to join a small group if you are not already in one. Each Sunday during these 40 days will be special times of worship related to the material and group study for the coming week. I encourage you to memorize, meditate. And put into practice the weekly memory verses, these are available to you in helping you develop a lifestyle of seeking God. My prayer is that God will be very real to you during these days and you will sense the need to go to God for everything. By doing so, you will experience the abundant and blessed life that God speaks of in His word, the Bible.

Our relationship to God is much more than what we can get out of God. You've heard the saying, "Well, I guess all we can do now is pray!" What we are really saying is that we have tried everything within our power and there is nothing else we can do so it is time to ask God to bail us out of a tough situation. When we say this is, we place God as a last resort and not as our first response. We try desperately in our own strength to "work it out." Our natural inclination is to do something — anything! Our culture also says, "Don't just sit there, do something!"

God eagerly wants to help us and bless us if we go to Him. God is much more concerned with His relationship with you than what things He can give you. We may be so focused on what God can do for us we fail to see the greatest blessing we could ever receive is God Himself. God wants to bless you beyond your wildest dreams! It all starts with coming to Him first.

It just makes sense that the Creator of the universe is the One we go to for everything. You may be discouraged in life thinking nothing will ever change because your past has dictated your present; your fear is preventing you from trying anything new. Look what God invites you to do, "Forget the former things; do not dwell on the past. See, I am doing a new thing! Now it springs up; do you not perceive it? I am making a way in the desert and streams in the wasteland. The wild animals honor me, the jackals and the owls, because I provide water in the desert and streams in the wasteland, to give drink to my people, my chosen, the people I formed for myself that they may proclaim my praise (Isaiah 43:18-21). God is going to make a way for you. If you have tried for years simply giving living without God, if you have found yourself growing stagnant or you simply have never prayed to God, He will make a way when you first go to God in prayer!

How do we begin going to God? Notice the verse at the top of this devotion, "Call to me and I will answer you and tell you great and unsearchable things you do not know" (Jeremiah 33:3). We need to call to Him and wait for God's answer. Ask Him — He will answer. Before you head into your next project, make a decision, draw up plans for the next "big thing", start by asking God! Learn from the Prophet Jeremiah, 'Not by might nor by power, but by my Spirit,' says the Lord Almighty (Zechariah 4:6). Too often, we plan and then ask God to bless what we are doing. It simply does not work that way. When we ask, we want to seek Him and know what God has to say and how He will direct us. To summarize how we begin going to God:

- Acknowledge God is real
- Ask God to be a part of your life
- Ask God what He would have you to do

As J. Oswald Sanders, the great prayer warrior says, "There is no way to learn to pray except by praying. No reasoned philosophy by itself ever taught a soul to pray." So then, let us start. Let's begin by developing the habit of turning to God as our first response. In the morning, whisper a short prayer as you begin your day and at the end of the day whisper a prayer as you go to bed. And during your day, as God reminds you, talk to Him as God prompts you.

POINT TO PONDER

Go to God first.

VERSE TO REMEMBER

The LORD is near to all who call on him, to all who call on him in truth. He fulfills the desires of those who fear him; he hears their cry and saves them. (Psalm 145:18-19)

QUESTION TO CONSIDER

How conscious are you of God in your life?

PRAYER FOCUS

Begin the day with a short prayer to God. Do the same before you sleep.

DAY 1 JOURNAL

_____

_____

_____

_____

_____

_____

_____

_____

_____

_____

_____

_____

_____

_____

Day 2

GOD IS INTO RELATIONSHIP

> *Here I am! I stand at the door and knock. If anyone hears my voice and opens the door, I will come in and eat with him, and he with me.*
> (Revelation 3:20)

Friends are fantastic! You depend on friends, confide in your friends, spend time with friends, and enjoy them simply because of who they are. And no matter how long you have known them or have spoken to them, you can always grow deeper in your relationship with them. The same goes with your relationship with God. As a matter of fact, God wants to deepen His relationship with you more than you do. It makes relationships so much sweeter when you know the person likes you, loves you and wants to spend more time with you.

God is so much into relationships that He tells us He looks everywhere for people who want to enter into a deeper relationship with Him, *The eyes of the LORD range throughout the earth to strengthen those whose hearts are fully committed to him.* (2 Chronicles 16:9) Ooh, did you catch the "C" word. Yes, God is looking for the committed. He's not looking for a flaky relationship or one that is "on again" and then "off again".

Yesterday, we talked about the development through these next 40 days of a habit — the lifestyle of seeking God. It is in response to what God is calling us to — relationship. God is already saying "yes" to us and we want to respond with a resounding "yes, God". Now, you might be thinking, "how committed is God?" He's so committed that He acted first in reaching out to us.

> *For he himself is our peace, who has made the two one and has destroyed the barrier, the dividing wall of hostility, by abolishing in his flesh the law with its commandments and regulations. His purpose was to create in himself one new man out of the two, thus making peace, and in this one body to reconcile both of them to God through the cross, by which he put to death their hostility. He came and preached peace to you who were far away and peace to those who were near. For through him we both have access to the Father by one Spirit.*
> (Ephesians 2:14-18)

Consider this, when someone really loves you it is not a matter of what you can do for them but just who you are. God loves you, not because you are lovable but because He chose to love you. His freedom stems from Jesus' victory on the cross and assures us that we can come before Him, warts and all. You see, God is holy and we are not. Jesus recognized this problem and died to pay for the wrongs in our lives. When we accept His forgiveness we are free from the performance trap that many of us have been living.

Those in this trap try to look good, and do good in order to "earn" the love and approval of others. When we don't live up to our expectations or the expectations of others, we feel we have failed. God saves us from this terrible ordeal by loving us even when we are far from perfect. He doesn't overlook our faults. That would be too trite and simplistic. He did what was necessary and sent Jesus to die and pay the price for our wrongs.

So, relax. God already knows all the wrongs in your life and your shortcomings. He made you in His image and gave you a sense of the eternal. If you have not done so, acknowledge what God has done for you. He loved you so much He died for you. He knew you even before you were born. He desires to have a relationship with you that is deep and meaningful. All you need to do is to trust in Him.

Since God desires a relationship with you, feel accepted. You simply need to approach Him honestly and acknowledge what He already knows. You can start with this suggested prayer. Read through this once and then pray it in your heart to God:

> "Dear Jesus, I have lived independent from you long enough. I know I am a sinner and need your forgiveness. I believe You died in my place and rose from the grave. I now trust You as my Lord and Savior. Thank you, Jesus for coming into my life. Forgive me of all my sin: past, present and future, and give me eternal life. In the strong and faithful name of Jesus I pray, amen."

If you prayed the above prayer and trusted Jesus from your heart, God assures you that your relationship with Him has just begun and He, as a faithful friend, will never leave you. You are a new person inside. God says you are now His child. Welcome to the family of God!

POINT TO PONDER

God desires an intimate relationship with you.

VERSE TO REMEMBER

For Christ died for sins once for all, the righteous for the unrighteous,
to bring you to God.
(1 Peter 3:18)

QUESTION TO CONSIDER

Do you have a vibrant relationship with God or
do you just know Him by name?

PRAYER FOCUS

Thank God He died for you and promises He will never leave you. Continue
to pray to God as you wake and before you sleep.

DAY 2 JOURNAL

_____

_____

_____

_____

_____

_____

_____

_____

_____

_____

_____

Day 3

SEEING FROM GOD'S VANTAGE POINT

> *For he (Abraham) was looking forward to the city with foundations,*
> *whose architect and builder is God.*
> (Hebrews 11:10)

We assess true value when we see through God's eyes.

"One man's junk is another man's treasure" is the garage sale seeker's, flea market shopper's motto. In the eyes of the world, the riches of God are often discarded, waiting for the one with the inspired eye to spot its true value. Take for instance, the most common of books, the Bible. The Bible is found in homes, hotels, given as gifts, cherished as family heirlooms and is the most printed book in the world. Yet, it is the one who gleans through God's Word with trained eyes that sees its true value.

How do we assess true value? Is it only that which has the highest price tag attached to it? Is it considered valuable only if something is rare? I can make a one of kind painting but who would consider it more than mere chicken scratch? It's got to be something more. Actually, God has a test: whatever endures the longest is the most valuable. Time, is a great litmus test for value. Those things that last forever are the most valuable. What are some of these things?

God points out several things that will last forever:

· God Himself is eternal
· People are eternal
· The Bible is eternal

Abraham was a man of great wealth but recognized his true riches surpassed his sheep, goats or lands he owned. He looked with eyes of faith and valued God. No wonder he is known as the "father of faith." He saw what many missed — that God was much more valuable than anything that eyes could see. With his enlightened eyes of faith, he recognized the things of God as true riches. In the same way, the Apostle Paul prayed for all believers to see the same thing.

> *I pray also that the eyes of your heart may be enlightened in order that you may know the hope to which he has called you, the riches of his glorious inheritance in the saints, and his incomparably great power for us who believe.*
> (Ephesians 1:18-19a)

When your eyes become enlightened, you are drawn to God because of His loveliness and beauty. You are caught in the awe of God and the things of God. When you see through God's eyes, your values change and are rightly aligned to eternal values.

God has come to show you what life is indeed. He beckons, "I have come that they may have life, and have it to the full". (John 10:10) He doesn't want you living out your life missing the true riches of life and focused on things that will not last. He wants you to have the most fulfilling life possible. The source of abundant life is God Himself. It is God that we need to prize and pursue. God invites us by asking, "Why spend money on what is not bread, and your labor on what does not satisfy? Listen, listen to me, and eat what is good, and your soul will delight in the richest of fare." (Isaiah 55:2) God is calling for us to see and delight in Him. He doesn't want you to waste another minute of your life on things that will not matter for eternity. Now, this does not mean we stop eating or working or shopping. What God wants is for us to delight in Him and then He will make everything in your life meaningful because you will see everything with an eternal perspective.

Jesus warns against following after what this world has to offer yet neglecting the soul. The key here is worldly perspective verses an eternal one. What good will it be for a man if he gains the whole world, yet forfeits his soul? Or what can a man give in exchange for his soul? (Matthew 16:26-27) Notice this is more than getting into heaven but it is about living on earth with an eternal view. No sense in wasting valuable time and energy on things that will not make a difference for eternity. The challenge for us today is to heed God's call to the eternal and spare us from things that "don't amount to a hill of beans" when all is said and done. When we see from God's vantage point, we too will be able to assess true value and live worthwhile lives.

POINT TO PONDER

We assess true value when we see through God's eyes.

VERSE TO REMEMBER

I lift up my eyes to you, to you whose throne is in heaven.
(Psalm 123:1)

QUESTION TO CONSIDER

How much of what you do will make an eternal difference?

PRAYER FOCUS

God help me to see with spiritual eyes.
Continue to pray in the morning and before you sleep.

DAY 3 JOURNAL

_____

_____

_____

_____

_____

_____

_____

_____

_____

_____

_____

_____

_____

_____

_____

_____

Day 4

IT'S A MATTER OF THE HEART

> Jesus replied: "'Love the Lord your God with all your heart and with all your soul and with all your mind.' This is the first and greatest commandment. And the second is like it: 'Love your neighbor as yourself.' All the Law and the Prophets hang on these two commandments."
> (Matthew 22:37-40)

Direct your heart Godward.

How does Almighty God tell us to love Him without coming across as forcing us to do something against our will? He wants us to come to Him willingly with our heart but we have a big problem. The Bible tells us how we are all wired, There is no one who understands, no one who seeks God (Romans 3:11). If we do not come to Him on our own then how is this possible?

God has to take the first step. God saw the problem — we could not come to Him on our own. We need His power in order to approach Him. He did away with the power that bound us and freed us through the death, burial and resurrection of Jesus. By Jesus conquering over death, Jesus broke the power and penalty of sin. We now can respond to Him because the Spirit of God lives within us.

God wants your heart not just your outward appearance, good church attendance, faithful tithing, or good intentions. God wants you! We can please God by many different actions; however none of those actions mean anything unless our hearts are engaged. It's like this, we can do many good things but if it is not for the Lord, it is nothing. Only what is done for God will last. Now it is possible because of Jesus' victory.

How then can we please God? We please God when we come to Him for who He is. Our heart is to love Him, spend time with Him and enjoy Him. We are prone to come to God only when we want something from Him. God wants us to come to Him just because of Him. The greatest command is, "Love, the Lord your God with all your heart" without condition. He wants us to learn what it is like to love as He loves. Besides, He has already given everything we need, His divine power has given us everything we need for life and godliness through our knowledge of him who called us by his own glory and goodness (2 Peter 1:3).

How do we love God with all our heart? We can learn from King David who is known as "a man after God's own heart." David spent time with God, learned the ways of God, developed a familiarity that led him know what God liked and did not like. The process started by simply listening to God and understanding His likes and dislikes. He noticed that God was righteous, just, loving, forgiving but also angry toward sin, the Devil, evildoers, injustice and those who were proud. Through time, David adopted God's attitude and thus had a heart attitude that was Godward.

During 40 Days of Prayer, pursue God with all of your heart. Learn to know Him, what He likes and dislikes. Appreciate His qualities and embrace what God embraces. You will find yourself loving God more and more and your heart will surge toward Him. The more time we spend in prayer, talking with God, understanding his thoughts, his ways, his purposes the more we will delight in the things of God.

People who are in love know what the other person's favorite color is, his favorite ice-cream, what he would do if he had free time, and what makes him laugh. When we love God, we want to acquaint ourselves with who God is and what He likes and what He is all about. How can we do this? Here are some things you can consider to pursue God with all your heart:

- Ask God to reveal His heart to you
- By faith, turn your heart to Him
- Familiarize yourself with His love letters, the Bible, to you.
- Adopt God's attitude as your own. Love what He loves and hate what He hates.

POINT TO PONDER

Direct your heart Godward.

VERSE TO REMEMBER

The LORD does not look at the things man looks at.
Man looks at the outward appearance, but the LORD looks at the heart.
(1 Samuel 16:7)

QUESTION TO CONSIDER

Do you ask what God wants or do you pray that God blesses what you do?

PRAYER FOCUS

Lord, change my heart to pursue after You throughout the day.
Continue to pray as you wake and before you sleep.

DAY 4 JOURNAL

_____

_____

_____

_____

_____

_____

_____

_____

_____

_____

_____

_____

_____

_____

_____

_____

_____

_____

Day 5

GOD IS MORE THAN ENOUGH!

> *But he said to me, "My grace is sufficient for you, for my power is made perfect in weakness."*
> *Therefore I will boast all the more gladly about my weaknesses,*
> *so that Christ's power may rest on me.*
> (2 Corinthians 12:9)

God is all we need.

God holds heaven and earth together and He knows what you need. He has promised to meet your needs and reminds us that He is all we need even when faced with incredible demands in life. By focusing on God, we will save ourselves from chasing after things and experiences in the name of meeting our needs when God says He will take care of us. Read with a sense of freedom this instruction from Jesus:

> [25]*"Therefore I tell you, do not worry about your life, what you will eat or drink; or about your body, what you will wear. Is not life more important than food, and the body more important than clothes?* [26]*Look at the birds of the air; they do not sow or reap or store away in barns, and yet your heavenly Father feeds them. Are you not much more valuable than they?* [27]*Who of you by worrying can add a single hour to his life?* [28]*And why do you worry about clothes? See how the lilies of the field grow. They do not labor or spin.* [29]*Yet I tell you that not even Solomon in all his splendor was dressed like one of these.* [30]*If that is how God clothes the grass of the field, which is here today and tomorrow is thrown into the fire, will he not much more clothe you, O you of little faith?* [31]*So do not worry, saying, 'What shall we eat?' or 'What shall we drink?' or 'What shall we wear?'* [32]*For the pagans run after all these things, and your heavenly Father knows that you need them* [33]*But seek first his kingdom and his righteousness, and all these things will be given to you as well.*
> (Matthew 6:25-33)

Jesus tells us to relax and trust Him with our needs and gives the antidote for worry — "seek first his kingdom and his righteousness" and you will get these other things too. God is more than enough. He wants to give us the very best — Himself.

When our attention shifts from the things of this world to the things of God we will know the freedom that Jesus speaks about. This happens when we pursue God, the source of all things. And when God responds by giving us His blessing, we need to respond by thanking Him. Every good and perfect gift is from above, coming down from the Father of the heavenly lights, who does not change like shifting shadows (James 1:17). What greater gift has come down from heaven than Jesus Himself? He is the Perfect Gift! When we realize we have all we need in Jesus, then God gets the attention and glory. We will not be able to boast in our great abilities, plans, positioning, cunning, or wisdom. It will all be unto the Lord; and it won't just be words but the truth. As a result, we will live out the value of coming to Him and spending time talking with Him.

How important is God's promise that He is sufficient for us? Without fully trusting God that He is sufficient, we will not give up our own ways or stop depending on things that will not last. We learn to trust in Him and know that He has everything we need for life when we let go of our own plans and depend on Him. Hear the testimony of King David when He relied completely on God,

O God, you are my God, earnestly I seek you; my soul thirsts for you, my body longs for you, in a dry and weary land where there is no water. I have seen you in the sanctuary and beheld your power and your glory. Because your love is better than life, my lips will glorify you. I will praise you as long as I live, and in your name I will lift up my hands. My soul will be satisfied as with the richest of foods; with singing lips my mouth will praise you.

(Psalm 63:1-5)

Here is a person who knows from experience, God is enough. Nothing else will satisfy us until we come to the place where God Himself is our sufficiency. How is God our sufficiency?

- He promises to supply all your needs.
  And my God will meet all your needs according to his glorious riches in Christ Jesus.
  (Philippians 4:19)
- He has saved your soul and given you eternal life.
  For you are receiving the goal of your faith, the salvation of your souls. (1 Peter 1:9)
- He has given you a hope and a future.
  For I know the plans I have for you," declares the LORD, "plans to prosper you and not to harm you, plans to give you hope and a future. Then you will call upon me and come and pray to me, and I will listen to you. You will seek me and find me when you seek me with all your heart. (Jeremiah 29:11-13)
- He will guide you throughout your life.
  Be strong and courageous. Do not be afraid or terrified because of them, for the LORD your God goes with you; he will never leave you nor forsake you. (Deuteronomy 31:6)

Rest assured, God is all you need!

POINT TO PONDER

God is all we need.

VERSE TO REMEMBER

Test me in this," says the Lord Almighty, "and see if I will not throw open the floodgates of heaven and pour out so much blessing that you will not have room enough for it.
(Malachi 3:10)

QUESTION TO CONSIDER

How can I practically trust God more today?

PRAYER FOCUS

Tell God you trust Him with what's on your heart. Continue to pray as you wake and before you sleep.

DAY 5 JOURNAL

_____

_____

_____

_____

_____

_____

_____

_____

_____

_____

_____

_____

Day 6

GOD'S CALL TO PRAY TOGETHER

> *"This, then, is how you should pray: "'Our Father in heaven, hallowed be your name.*
> (Matthew 6:9)

God's power comes when we pray together.

In our society we value rugged individualism. We have images of the Marlboro man riding off to the sunset on his faithful steed as everyone looks admiringly at his silhouette against the setting sun. It's a romantic idea we have in America that if someone puts his mind to it, if only a person tries hard enough, he can accomplish anything. God has another idea though that is much more glorious. He longs for the day when we come to Him together. We don't need to be a collection of spiritual superstars but together we can do more than any one person can accomplish.

Notice the above verse from Matthew 6:9. They are familiar words and begin the Lord's Prayer, the most famous prayer in the world. As Jesus instructed His disciples to pray, He begins with the word, "Our". If we were to continue through the prayer, it is clear that the emphasis is on them praying together, not individually. Certainly, we ought to pray by ourselves but there is a blessing and power that only comes when we pray together. For the most part, the majority of the New Testament was written to whole group of believers and not individuals. When we are exhorted to live out the Christian life, we are encouraged to do it together and not in separate worlds. Even in the imagery of Jesus as our Shepherd, points to us coming together. One thing about sheep is that they like to wander but it is the task of the shepherd to gather them together. It's His desire yet our natural inclination is to separate and go our own way. He has a special promise when we come together and pray to Him. 19"Again, I tell you that if two of you on earth agree about anything you ask for, it will be done for you by my Father in heaven. 20For where two or three come together in my name, there am I with them." (Matthew 18:19)

As believers, we long for revival and the Spirit of God to move with power — freely among His people. One "requirement" or "sign" before this takes place is the coming together of God's people to call on Him.

> *The Lord appeared to him at night and said: "I have heard your prayer and have chosen this place for myself as a temple for sacrifices. "When I shut up the heavens so that there is no rain, or command locusts to devour the land or send a plague among my people, if my people, who are called by my name, will humble themselves and pray and seek my face and turn from their wicked ways, then will I hear from heaven and will forgive their sin and will heal their land. Now my eyes will be open and my ears attentive to the prayers offered in this place. I have chosen and consecrated this temple so that my Name may be there forever. My eyes and my heart will always be there.*
>
> (2 Chronicles 7:12-16)

The power of God comes when the people of God gather together to pray.

Have you been a Lone Ranger Christian? When was the last time you prayed with a group of believers? God calls us to come together because it brings people in agreement with Himself. If you've been struggling in your prayer life and wondered how it can develop, it just might be that you need to be a part of a vibrant group of believers who pour their hearts out to God.

When do we gather together to seek God?

- On the Lord's Day
  There are six days when you may work, but the seventh day is a Sabbath of rest, a day of sacred assembly. You are not to do any work; wherever you live, it is a Sabbath to the LORD. (Leviticus 23:3)
- As the church gathers — Fresh Encounter (Our corporate prayer gathering)
  And pray in the Spirit on all occasions with all kinds of prayers and requests. With this in mind, be alert and always keep on praying for all the saints. (Ephesians 6:18)
- Special times of prayer
  Declare a holy fast; call a sacred assembly. Summon the elders and all who live in the land to the house of the LORD your God, and cry out to the LORD. (Joel 1:14)

POINT TO PONDER

God's power comes when we pray together.

VERSE TO REMEMBER

For where two or three come together in my name, there am I with them." (Matthew 18:20)

QUESTION TO CONSIDER

How can you be more involved in praying with others?

PRAYER FOCUS

Seek out one other person to pray with today.
Continue to pray when you awake and before you sleep.

DAY 6 JOURNAL

_____

_____

_____

_____

_____

_____

_____

_____

_____

_____

_____

_____

_____

_____

_____

_____

_____

_____

_____

_____

Day 7

A HOLY ASSEMBLY: BECOMING A HOUSE OF PRAYER

> *"Then will I purify the lips of the peoples, that all of them may call on the name of the Lord and serve him shoulder to shoulder.*
> (Zephaniah 3:9)

God calls us to be holy.

When we think of Jesus, we think of Him as kind, gentle, understanding, loving, mild and meek. That's what makes the accounts of Jesus getting angry so extraordinary. He taught everyone to forgive and show temperance. What could have set Him off? Once during the beginning of his ministry and another at the end of his ministry, Jesus went to the temple to worship only to find commerce had overrun the temple. The place was operating like a marketplace. Read the short account, Jesus entered the temple area and drove out all who were buying and selling there. He overturned the tables of the money changers and the benches of those selling doves. "It is written," he said to them, "'My house will be called a house of prayer,' but you are making it a 'den of robbers.'" (Matthew 21:12-13). Jesus saw what happened to God's house, it was turned into a place to make a fast buck. Their focus was not on worship or providing a needful service to the people but in taking advantage of the requirements for the people to come to God with a sacrifice. In essence, they ran religious concession stands and the people had no choice but to pay up. In doing so, they diminished the temple of God into a marketplace. Jesus cries out, "It is written," he said to them, "'My house will be a house of prayer'; but you have made it 'a den of robbers.'" (Luke 19:46). His response, turning over the tables and driving out the people gives us a picture of the severity of the situation and calls for holiness to be restored to God's house.

Interestingly, Jesus calls the temple, God's house of prayer. Jesus quotes Isaiah, These I will bring to my holy mountain and give them joy in my house of prayer. Their burnt offerings and sacrifices will be accepted on my altar; for my house will be called a house of prayer for all nations. (Isaiah 56:7). It is not to be known as a place of singing, preaching, service, sacrifice, or tithing, although those activities will take place. It is to be known as a house of prayer. What distinguishes a place as a place of prayer and one that simply prays? Notice what Fred. A. Hartley III observed between "a church that prays" and "a church devoted to prayer".

A CHURCH THAT PRAYS	A CHURCH DEVOTED TO PRAYER
1. Prays about what it does.	1. Does things by prayer.
2. Fits prayer in.	2. Gives prayer priority.
3. Prays when there are problems.	3. Prays when there are opportunities.
4. Announces a special time of prayer — some in the church show up.	4. Announces a special time of prayer — the entire church shows up.
5. Asks God to bless what it is doing.	5. Asks God to enable it to do what He is blessing.
6. Is frustrated by financial shortfall — backs down from projects.	6. Is challenged by financial shortfall — calls for fasting, prayer, and faith.
7. Is tired, weary, stressed out.	7. Mounts up with wings like eagles, runs and doesn't grow weary, walks and does not faint.
8. Does things within its means.	8. Does things beyond its means.
9. Sees its members as its parish.	9. Sees the world as its parish.
10. Is involved in the work of man	10. Is involved in the work of God.

The church that neglects prayer lacks the spiritual power to excel while the church devoted to prayer excels because God honors what he has established as the top priority in His house. The church devoted to prayer has set itself apart as holy unto the Lord.

How can your life be a holy "House of God"?

· Develop a holy fear of the Lord
Therefore, since we are receiving a kingdom that cannot be shaken, let us be thankful, and so worship God acceptably with reverence and awe, for our "God is a consuming fire." (Hebrews 12:28-29)

· Clear all idols from your life
"If you will return, O Israel, return to me," declares the Lord. "If you put your detestable idols out of my sight and no longer go astray, and if in a truthful, just and righteous way you swear, 'As surely as the Lord lives,' then the nations will be blessed by him and in him they will glory." This is what the Lord says to the men of Judah and to Jerusalem: "Break up your unplowed ground and do not sow among thorns. Circumcise yourselves to the Lord, circumcise your hearts, you men of Judah and people of Jerusalem, or my wrath will break out and burn like fire because of the evil you have done — burn with no one to quench it. (Jeremiah 4:1-4)

· Remember who you were
All of us have become like one who is unclean, and all our righteous acts are like filthy rags; we all shrivel up like a leaf, and like the wind our sins sweep us away (Isaiah 64:6)

- Pray at all times

Pray continually (1 Thessalonians 5:17)

- Keep your worship pure

For it is we who are the circumcision, we who worship by the Spirit of God, who glory in Christ Jesus, and who put no confidence in the flesh (Philippians 3:3)

POINT TO PONDER

God calls us to be holy.

VERSE TO REMEMBER

"It is written," he said to them, "'My house will be called a house of prayer.'" (Matthew 21:13)

QUESTION TO CONSIDER

How can you be more involved in God's vision for the church, "a house of prayer"?

PRAYER FOCUS

How can you display holiness today? Pray as you awake and before you sleep each day through the remainder of 40 days.

DAY 7 JOURNAL

_____

_____

_____

_____

_____

_____

_____

_____

Pray for God's Pleasure

Day 8

IT'S ALL ABOUT THE LORD

> Give thanks to the LORD, call on his name; make known among the nations what he has done. Sing to him, sing praise to him; tell of all his wonderful acts. Glory in his holy name; let the hearts of those who seek the Lord rejoice. Look to the Lord and his strength; seek his face always. Remember the wonders he has done, his miracles, and the judgments he pronounced.
>
> (1 Chronicles 16:8-12)

God deserves our worship.

How on earth can we please God? It's the theme for our 40 Days and also the topic for today. If God is perfect, holy and all-together sufficient, why does he want us to pray to Him? Does He really need our prayers? Would they be missed? What difference do our prayers make?

No, God does not need our prayers but He delights in them.

> I urge, then, first of all, that requests, prayers, intercession and thanksgiving be made for everyone — for kings and all those in authority, that we may live peaceful and quiet lives in all godliness and holiness. This is good, and pleases God our Savior.
>
> (1 Timothy 2:1-3)

Our prayers are cherished by God and carefully kept.

> And when he had taken it, the four living creatures and the twenty-four elders fell down before the Lamb. Each one had a harp and they were holding golden bowls full of incense, which are the prayers of the saints,
>
> (Revelation 5:8)

And yes, our prayers do matter. Our prayers literally move heaven and earth!

> I will give you the keys of the kingdom of heaven; whatever you bind on earth will be bound in heaven, and whatever you loose on earth will be loosed in heaven.
>
> (Matthew 16:19)

Read that last verse again! Your prayers have more impact than you can imagine. Only if we come together and pray— God will do it!

We please God when we align ourselves with what He is all about. He has told us His heart is for everyone to come and know Him. He has also revealed to us that we need to honor Him at all times and live a life worthy of the call of God. We bring pleasure to God when we pray according to what He has revealed concerning His heart.

We pray to God because it pleases Him and because He deserves it. If God did nothing else in your life, He would still be worthy of all your worship, praise and prayer. When we arrive at the realization of this truth we know we are at the beginning of true worship. When we worship not because He needs us but because He deserves it and we need Him, we begin to truly pray. We approach Him because we delight in Him. We gain much more from prayer than God does. We please Him by our prayers and through them we receive great blessing.

POINT TO PONDER

God deserves our worship.

VERSE TO REMEMBER

Great is the LORD and most worthy of praise;
his greatness no one can fathom.
(Psalm 145:3)

QUESTION TO CONSIDER

What will you pray about today to please God?

PRAYER FOCUS

You can move heaven and earth with your prayers.
What will you pray about today?

DAY 8 JOURNAL

Day 9

SEEKING THE LORD

> God looks down from heaven on the sons of men to see
> if there are any who understand, any who seek God.
> (Psalm 53:2)

Seek God's heart.

The Wizard of Oz asked Dorothy and her friends, "What do you want?" The Scarecrow wanted a brain, the Tin Man wanted a heart, the Cowardly Lion wanted courage, and Dorothy longed for Kansas, her home. It's quite telling how we answer the same question today, "What do you want?" Some may be content with material blessing; others with power; some with fame; and still others with good health. And some long for the heart's true home, God Himself.

It is not wrong to seek for things, blessings or accomplishments. Yet, the order in our seeking is important. When we seek God for who He is first, He will give us what we need - Himself, and also additional blessings. But seek first his kingdom and his righteousness, and all these things will be given to you as well (Matthew 6:33). When we seek God first we bring delight to God's heart. As a parent, some of the greatest moments come when my children come to me and they do not want anything from me. They only want to spend time with me, sit on my lap and be near dad. God also delights when we come just to be near Him.

King David could have asked God for many things but this is the one thing He wanted, One thing I ask of the LORD, this is what I seek: that I may dwell in the house of the LORD all the days of my life, to gaze upon the beauty of the LORD and to seek him in his temple (Psalm 27:4). Now, here was a man who was a king, warrior, and shepherd but also one who was sensitive to God, a seeker of God, and a lover of God. Sure he wanted conquests, rule more lands, more soldiers, more weaponry, but His greatest desire was for God Himself. He was a man of prayer, a man that sought God.

David sought "God's face" before "God's hand." That is, he went to God for who He was and not for what He could get out of God. He did not want to cheapen his relationship with God but honor Him. David, a man of war, conquest, revered as king yet God noted what really set him apart, David son of Jesse a man after my own heart; he will do everything I want him to do (Acts 13:22). In God's eyes, what set him apart was that he sought God to the point he adopted God's heart and his obedience to God. David comments about his relationship with God, I saw the Lord always before me. Because he is at my right hand, I will not be shaken (Acts 2:25). His seeking of God became a lifestyle. David's spiritual life blossomed to the point where he knew God was "right before" him. It was as if he could reach out his hand and touch Him.

Here's the key. David's seeking after God was not a side habit but a satisfying lifestyle, developed through an intimate relationship. He delighted in God, loved God and wanted to serve Him. His seeking God was a direct link and cause to his successes on the battlefield. When he sought God, he prospered. When he left God, he diminished. God blessed David because of his heart transformation.

What can you do to seek God today?

- Seek God for who He is. Spend a moment in silence before Him.
- Acknowledge that He is God and you are his child.
- Ask God to reveal His heart to you.

The poor will see and be glad — you who seek God, may your hearts live!
(Psalm 69:32)

POINT TO PONDER

Seek God's heart.

VERSE TO REMEMBER

You will seek me and find me when you seek me with all your heart.
(Jeremiah 29:13)

QUESTION TO CONSIDER

"What do you want?" Is it God Himself? If not, why?

PRAYER FOCUS

Seek God as if your life depended on it — because it does.

DAY 9 JOURNAL

Day 10

DRAWING TOWARD THE LORD

> *Let us then approach the throne of grace with confidence,*
> *so that we may receive mercy and find grace to help us in our time of need.*
> (Hebrews 4:16)

God invites us to boldly come to Him.

In ancient times, rulers were generally unapproachable by the common people. Some would not even allow their highest ranking officials to come without permission. Queen Esther risked her life in approaching King Ahasuerus without invitation, even though she was his wife! Nehemiah risked his life by coming before King Artaxerxes with a sad face and he was his cupbearer. God has removed all the barriers through Christ's sacrifice on the cross. Instead of a throne of judgment, we can now come to God's throne of grace.

It's the throne of grace because here God freely gives out his grace. He tells us to come boldly; don't be shy. It may seem too good to be true but it is not. It's God's invitation to you and me. When we draw near to Him, God gives us much in return. From yesterday's reading, we know that seeking God for who He is comes first; as a result though, God showers His blessings upon us. Then, how much should you pray or ask? It depends on how much you want to be blessed! Here's the principle:

Much prayer, much blessing; little prayer, little blessing; no prayer, no blessing.

It comes from the agricultural principle of sowing and reaping. Remember this: Whoever sows sparingly will also reap sparingly, and whoever sows generously will also reap generously (2 Corinthians 9:6). If you want abundant blessing in your life, draw near to God. Cling to Him as if your life depends on it. Jesus, as our High Priest, knows exactly what we need. When we draw near to Him, he understands our situation and will meet our needs. The more we come to Him, the more He will bless us.

When we stand at a distance we miss out on much that God has for us. When we timidly come before Him, we miss out because we are not likely to ask of Him. No, when we come to Him boldly we are more likely to receive because we come believing in His promise, And without faith it is impossible to please God, because anyone who comes to him must believe that he exists and that he rewards those who earnestly seek him (Hebrews 11:6). Come boldly, come confidently, come to God often and he will reward you.

God does not want us to live at a distant. He wants us to walk closely, intimately with Him through life. Drawing near does not mean we physically move closer to Him or that we somehow move from one place to another. Drawing near to God involves the heart. It is a heart movement toward God. When you take a step toward God, He will come closer to you. He promises, Come near to God and he will come near to you. Wash your hands, you sinners, and purify your hearts, you double-minded (James 4:8). As we come to God in prayer, we cannot help but be drawn closer to Him. Our drawing near to God is based on what God has already accomplished.

- God made it possible for you to come to Him
  For Christ died for sins once for all, the righteous for the unrighteous, to bring you to God. He was put to death in the body but made alive by the Spirit. (1 Peter 3:18)
- Through Jesus we now have peace with God
  Therefore, since we have been justified through faith, we have peace with God through our Lord Jesus Christ. (Romans 5:1)

God wants to give us abundant life here on earth. It pleases Him when we draw near him. It's more than a command; it is an invitation, and permission to come before God. When we do, we experience God Himself and all that He has for us. The barriers have been broken; the way is made plain; we can now come to God — so come boldly, often and with delight before the throne of grace.

Therefore he is able to save completely those who come to God through him,
because he always lives to intercede for them.
(Hebrews 7:25)

POINT TO PONDER

God invites us to boldly come to Him.

VERSE TO REMEMBER

Let us then approach the throne of grace with confidence, so that we may receive mercy and find grace to help us in our time of need.
(Hebrews 4:16)

QUESTION TO CONSIDER

Would you turn down an invitation from God?

PRAYER FOCUS

Much prayer, much blessing; little prayer, little blessing; no prayer, no blessing.

DAY 10 JOURNAL

_____

_____

_____

_____

_____

_____

_____

_____

_____

_____

_____

_____

_____

_____

_____

_____

_____

Day 11

RESTING IN THE LORD

> *My soul finds rest in God alone; my salvation comes from him. He alone is my rock and my salvation; he is my fortress, I will never be shaken.*
> (Psalm 62:1-2)

You can rest when you know God is in control.

For the last several months, a popular car ad has run on television showing a man grinning and saying, "Drive? I like to drive." He has the look of a man that loves control and he can't wait to get behind the wheel of that monster car and control it. We love the thrill of going down the slopes full speed when we ski, giving it your all in your job or even taking life by the horns in your life. All these things, we feel we have some level of control; and as long as everything feels like it is in our power, we are fine. It's only when we...lose control that we begin to wonder, begin to doubt, question and when the thrills become frightening.

Certain activities are better left to the experts such as flying an airplane, performing internal surgery, or building a building. Yet, I'm perfectly content in being a passenger in the plane, going under the knife, or comfortably sit in the lobby when I have faith in the person or persons in control, the ones who know what they are doing.

Ultimately, this is carried over into life itself. We may feel we are qualified but it may turn out to get a little bumpy and downright out of control. Life can come across as tame one moment and look quite ferocious the next. When life is given over to God, we can feel relaxed. The God of the Ages is in control and everything is going to be fine. Now, this is not about abdicating personal responsibility but about ultimate control in your life and mine.

When we rest in God and do what He would have us to do, everything goes well. Listen to God's plea toward us, Oh, that their hearts would be inclined to fear me and keep all my commands always, so that it might go well with them and their children forever! (Deuteronomy 5:29). Like the ones sitting on an airplane, we can wrestle the wheel back or relax knowing God is piloting the plane of our life just fine. It's a choice we need to make each day.

Notice that whether it is an airplane, car, motorcycle, bicycle or your life, it just does not make sense for two people to steer. The ride is so much smoother if one is in control. If we struggle with God for control, the direction of our lives will waver and turn here and there. We might even take back control once in awhile only to find that we are out of control. We could turn back to him at such times and He if faithful to steer us back on course. In fact, we find that God does such a great job of leading our lives; we should give Him control all the time! It is much better simply to have God, with capable hands, directing the ride of our lives.

King David found that wrestling with God for control is not the answer. Completely relaxed, having God in charge is the solution.

Find rest, O my soul, in God alone; my hope comes from him. He alone is my rock and my salvation; he is my fortress, I will not be shaken. My salvation and my honor depend on God; he is my mighty rock, my refuge. Trust in him at all times, O people; pour out your hearts to him, for God is our refuge.

(Psalm 62:5-8)

How can you relax in God today?

- It's a trust issue. Do you believe God has your best interest at heart?
- It's a faith issue. Will you let Him continue even when you don't know where He is leading you?
- It's a submission issue. Will you let God control/direct your life?

POINT TO PONDER

You can rest when you know God is in control.

VERSE TO REMEMBER

(Jesus invites) "Come to me, all you who are weary and burdened, and I will give you rest. Take my yoke upon you and learn from me, for I am gentle and humble in heart, and you will find rest for your souls. For my yoke is easy and my burden is light."
(Matthew 11:28-30)

QUESTION TO CONSIDER

Do you trust God to be in control until you reach your final destination, heaven?

PRAYER FOCUS

What area of your life needs to be given over to God's control?

DAY 11 JOURNAL

_____

_____

_____

_____

_____

_____

_____

_____

_____

_____

_____

_____

_____

_____

_____

_____

_____

_____

_____

_____

_____

_____

_____

_____

_____

_____

Day 12

WAITING ON THE LORD

> *Even youths grow tired and weary, and young men stumble and fall; but those who hope in the Lord will renew their strength. They will soar on wings like eagles; they will run and not grow weary, they will walk and not be faint.*
> (Isaiah 40:30-31)

Waiting is worthwhile when it is on the Lord.

Nobody likes delays! Nobody! We live in a society that is into fast, fast, fast! The oven must have been the toast of the town when it became a household item — imagine cooking a whole chicken in under an hour! Then came the microwave — sure it's frozen but give it 5 or 10 minutes and you can get a hot meal. For some that is still too long — so they invented the fast food chicken joint. Chicken boiled, seasoned to perfection waiting for your order and delivered to you while you drive through!

We have scheduled our lives, automated our appliances, and optimized the time it takes for each task of the day that if one or two items are delayed, look out. In such a fast, efficient oriented society, God wants our attention and He wants us to slow down. Why, because He does not want us to be more productive? Hardly. He has ordained a God-given rhythm to life that will produce the greatest joy and fulfillment in life. For starters, He has ordained for us to work six days and to keep the Lord's Day holy, For in six days the LORD made the heavens and the earth, the sea, and all that is in them, but he rested on the seventh day. Therefore the LORD blessed the Sabbath day and made it holy (Exodus 20:11). When we abide by God's law, we flourish. When we violate it, we become weary and disoriented towards life.

He wants to help us slow down enough for uus to come to Him for who He is. "Be still, and know that I am God; I will be exalted among the nations, I will be exalted in the earth" (Psalm 46:10). By waiting on God we attribute several honorable attitudes toward God:

God has the right answers.

- God has the right questions.
- God has the right timing.
- God has the right resources.
- God has the right!

We please God when we wait on Him; and we benefit when we wait. We don't end up being more behind; we end up ahead when He answers.

Waiting on the Lord is for all occasions, particularly during the mundane issues surrounding living. In the morning, O LORD, you hear my voice; in the morning I lay my requests before you and wait in expectation (Psalm 5:3). It is needed for daily living. Nothing is tougher than going through the routines of life. Sure nobody looks forward to the tough times but usually they are few and far between. It is the daily normal activities of life that can cause great ruts.

When we wait on the Lord, He gives us what we need and equips us for further work. Dr. Henry Blackaby notes, "God never told men to do something they could do on their own." When we wait on the Lord, He reveals impossibility in our eyes that can be accomplished through His strength. Waiting also humbles us and draws our attention toward God. It directs us away from our problems, circumstances of life, to our Savior who leads us through each obstacle. Here is how the waiting on the Lord in prayer works:

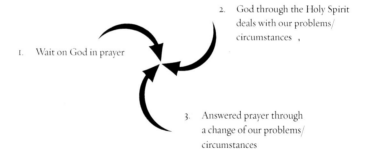

2. God through the Holy Spirit deals with our problems/circumstances ,

1. Wait on God in prayer

3. Answered prayer through a change of our problems/circumstances

By waiting on God, we are able to present life's problems/circumstances and be still enough to notice God is the one that deals with them and changes them. He may change the heart of others, open or close doors of opportunity, and numerous other answers to prayer. This is not to say we do nothing but our first response is to God. He will direct us toward any action. Let God speak to you, The LORD will fight for you; you need only to be still (Exodus 14:14). We can be completely relaxed when we wait on the Lord, knowing He has our best at heart and He fights for us!

POINT TO PONDER

Waiting is worthwhile when it is on the Lord.

VERSE TO REMEMBER

Wait for the LORD; be strong and take heart and wait for the LORD. (Psalm 27:14)

QUESTION TO CONSIDER

What area do you need God to fight for you today?

PRAYER FOCUS

Are you willing to wait on God's timetable and not put a time restriction on Him?

DAY 12 JOURNAL

_____

_____

_____

_____

_____

_____

_____

_____

_____

_____

_____

_____

_____

_____

Day 13

INTIMACY WITH THE LORD

> *"Abraham believed God, and it was credited to him as righteousness," and he was called God's friend.*
> (James 2:23)

Intimacy with God is not automatic but is nurtured.

You know you've got a good friend when they know all about you — and love you anyway! But in order to get to that point, they have to get to know all about you, your weaknesses, your dirty laundry, skeletons in the closet and annoying habits.

We've got a great head start developing intimacy with God. He already knows all the junk in our lives — and He still loves us! It's our response to Him that is limiting the level of intimacy. You see, God is waiting, desperately waiting for us to acknowledge what He knows about us. He's waiting for us to open our hearts to Him fully. He won't be surprised. He won't shrink back thinking how weird we are.

You might be thinking, "Is an intimate relationship with God Almighty even possible?" Some ordinary people developed an intimate relationship with God found in Scripture for us to examine. These were ordinary people that simply trusted in an extraordinary God.

- Enoch
  Enoch walked with God; then he was no more, because God took him away.
  (Genesis 5:24)
- Job
  How I long for the months gone by, for the days when God watched over me, when his lamp shone upon my head and by his light I walked through darkness! Oh, for the days when I was in my prime, when God's intimate friendship blessed my house. (Job 29:2-4)
- Abraham
  "Abraham believed God, and it was credited to him as righteousness," and he was called God's friend. (James 2:23)
- Moses
  Since then, no prophet has risen in Israel like Moses, whom the LORD knew face to face.

(Deuteronomy 34:10)

· Paul

I want to know Christ and the power of his resurrection and the fellowship of sharing in his sufferings, becoming like him in his death. (Philippians 3:10)

These individuals, many we consider saints and great models of the faith were not always that way. They were used of God as they developed their relationship with Him. Their intimacy level with God grew as they nourished their relationships with God and out of that came great deeds accomplished in God's Name. Notice the language used to describe the intimacy with God: walked, believed, friend, face to face, and to know.

These saints were not born but made. What can we learn from their relationships with God?

· Intimacy involves time
· Intimacy involves knowing the heart of the other
· Intimacy involves openness/transparency
· Intimacy involves daily communion/communication

You may notice that the above sounds a lot like a description of a couple in love; and you would be right. Our relationship with God is a lot like that. But it is much deeper. Drs. Les & Leslie Parrott, author of Relationships write, "Without an authentic relationship with God, we are left empty and detached. There is in all of us, at the very center of our lives, a burning in our heart that is deep and insatiable. Most often we try to quench that yearning with a human relationship. We try to fill the gap in our existence with a friend or lover. But no human relationship — no matter how wonderful — can ever complete us." We were made to have an intimate relationship with God, our Maker."

I remember when Andrea and I were dating, and by the way, we still do every Monday, we would look forward to our dates and I would have them marked in my calendar. We've gotten to the point where we have set as a priority every Monday to spend time together. Daily we also set aside time as well and communicate with each other throughout the day. It is the same with our relationship with God. Set a "date" with God where just the two of you can spend time together nurturing your relationship. Make it daily; make it a habit.

You may ask, "What would I do if I had so much time with God?" Here are some ideas from noted author John Eldredge, author of Wild At Heart, "Time with God each day is not about academic study or getting through a certain amount of Scripture or any of that. It's about connecting with God. We've got to keep those lines of communication open, so use whatever helps. Sometimes I'll listen to music; other times I'll read Scripture or a passage from a book;

often I will journal; maybe I'll go for a run; then there are days when all I need is silence and solitude and the rising sun. The point is simply to do whatever brings me back to my heart and the heart of God."

You've got your Bible, go ahead and use it. You've got this devotional — keep going through all 40 Days. You may have some great worship music that helps you connect with God. Go ahead and listen to it and let your soul be nourished and drawn to Him. These tools can assist you in nourishing your relationship with God. And you have the precious tool of prayer — pray anywhere and at anytime to your friend, Savior and Lord, Jesus Christ.

POINT TO PONDER

Intimacy with God is not automatic but is developed.

VERSE TO REMEMBER

I keep asking that the God of our Lord Jesus Christ, the glorious Father, may give you the Spirit of wisdom and revelation, so that you may know him better. (Ephesians 1:17)

QUESTION TO CONSIDER

How will you cultivate your relationship with Jesus today?

PRAYER FOCUS

Have a two-way conversation with God. He speaks through the Holy Spirit and the Bible. Respond to what He says to you.

DAY 13 JOURNAL

_____

_____

_____

_____

_____

_____

_____

Day 14

LOVING THE LORD

> We love because he first loved us.
> (1 John 4:19)

Loving God is a daily choice.

Loving God is an easy choice when we understand how great God's love is toward us. God loves us so much that He sent Jesus to die for the world — that includes you and me (John 3:16). God loved us even when we did not know Him. He loved us when we blew it and He loves us when we do well. To get a glimpse at how great God's love is, let's look at different types of love. Love is also a widely used term in our society that takes on many meanings. For instance, "I love ice cream" or "I love my dog". What does a person mean when they say, "I love sports," "I love Tuesdays," or "You've got to love it." My personal favorite in high school was "I love corduroy pants". When we see how far short the other types of love are, we can fully appreciate when God says, "I love you".

The Greeks had four words they used for love:

- *Phileo*, is at the root of Philadelphia, the city of brotherly love. This type of love is the "do good to me and I'll treat you right" type of love. It's "I'll scratch your back if you scratch my back" type of love. It is reciprocal in nature and quite cordial.
- *Eros*, the root of erotic is the appreciation of all that is created — like the beauty of the sunset or of a bird in flight. It is soulful and can tend toward the flesh.
- *Storge* or love of the family is a love stemming from relationships to those in our own household. It is the type of love that "keeps a promise" and is closely related to loyalty.
- *Agape* is God's type of love; it is unconditional. This type of love, loves because one chooses to love and not because of any inherent goodness in the object. That is, a person can love even when a person

has not done anything good or deserving of love. It is the opposite of the reward system. Agape loves in spite of the flaws seen in people or things. It looks for the possibility of what can be.

It's easy to love God when we understand He loves us with agape love. He has loved us from the very beginning and does not stop loving us when we mess up. He loves us when we were His enemies, For if, when we were God's enemies, we were reconciled to him through the death of his Son, how much more, having been reconciled, shall we be saved through his life! (Romans 5:10). He continues to love us because it is His nature to love. Now, this does not mean that everything in life will be smooth or comfortable. God loves us too much for us to drift off into mindlessness. He loves us so he disciplines us, strengthens us through trials, teaches us through failings and lifts us up when we fall. No wonder it is so easy to love God — He loves us without limit!

You and I cannot rightly love in our own strength. Your love and my love are not good enough! How can that be? Consider this; if we were to love God with Phileo love we would only love Him as we sense His love toward us. If we love Him with Eros love, we would only love Him if we acknowledged the wonders of His works. If we loved with Storge love, it would depend on how close we feel we were to God. The kind of love God is looking for is His kind of love, agape. The source of this type of love is from God. We cannot conjure up this love. When we allow God to control our lives more and more, agape love will be a by-product in our lives, resulting from the fruit of the Spirit (Galatians 5:22).

If we are to love God, it comes from the indwelling Spirit and movement of God within us to empower us to love in a supernatural way — it goes beyond our own capacity to love. Consider His command to love, And so we know and rely on the love God has for us. God is love. Whoever lives in love lives in God, and God in him (1 John 4:16). We are able to love with the highest form of love to the degree that God dwells within us. It's not an issue of salvation but an issue of how much have you and I allowed God to take control of our lives.

We love God because He is worthy. He is holy; He is our Savior; He is our Lord; He is our King. When we love God with agape style love, it does not depend on what He has done for us lately — although He continues to shower us with His blessings each day. It does not depend upon the beauty of the creation around us. We could be caught in the fog for several weeks and then what? We do not love Him based on how close we feel we are to Him at the moment. What would happen if we just did not feel like loving Him? What if our decision began to wane and we decided to take a break! No, the only way to love God, with His kind of love is with agape love, the type of love that loves no matter what. Whether we feel like or not; see His goodness in the moment or not; emotionally into it or not — we love Him because He first loved us!

Loving God, in the Scriptures is more than a warm fuzzy. God's definition of a person who loves God is someone who obeys what He says:

Whoever has my commands and obeys them, he is the one who loves me. He who loves me will be loved by my Father, and I too will love him and show myself to him ... If anyone loves me, he will obey my teaching. My father will love him, and we will come to him and make our home with him.
(John 14:21, 23)

"We shall all feel very much ashamed if we do not yield to Jesus on the point He has asked us to yield to Him ... To get there is a question of will, not of debate nor of reasoning, but a surrender of will, an absolute and irrevocable surrender on that point ... Obey God in the thing he shows you, and instantly the next thing is opened up. God will never reveal more truth about himself until you have obeyed what you know already."
(Oswald Chambers)

POINT TO PONDER

Loving God is a daily choice.

VERSE TO REMEMBER

Love the LORD your God with all your heart and with all your soul and with all your strength.
(Deuteronomy 6:5)

QUESTION TO CONSIDER

What type of love describes your love for God?

PRAYER FOCUS

Tell God how much you love Him.

DAY 14 JOURNAL

_____

_____

_____

_____

Pray for Outreach

Day 15

RECEIVING GOD'S HEART FOR THE LOST

This is good, and pleases God our Savior, who wants all men to be saved
and to come to a knowledge of the truth.
(1 Timothy 2:3-4)

God wants everyone to be saved.

Someone prayed for you before you came to Jesus. If you have not come to Jesus yet, there are many praying that you will. No one is looking forward to you coming to God more than God Himself. He wants that to be a reality so much that He has sent the church out on a mission that will not end until every single last person comes to know Him.

One of the most intense moments Jesus had here on earth occurred while He was praying to God the Father. Knowing that His time on earth was coming to an end, He prayed for the disciples and also for those who will believe in the future. *My prayer is not for them alone. I pray also for those who will believe in me through their message, that all of them may be one.* (John 17:20-21a) His heart was for all to come to know Him and receive forgiveness and God's love. And the vehicle in which the message would go out would not be through miraculous signs in the sky or numerous angelic visits, the message would spread by those who already believed. Also, he prayed that new believers would have the same heart as the older believers, meaning they would also adopt their heart, which was a reflection of God's heart for the lost.

And so the process continues down to this day. We are to carry on what has been entrusted to us. God will not stop loving, caring and wanting others to come to know Him until time itself is no more. If that is God's heart, we must also adopt His attitude toward those who do not yet know Him. To seek God and know Him more deeply is more than a personal journey of growth and satisfaction in this world, it is the adoption of attitudes and actions God would have us live out.

I realize for the most part, evangelism is seen as a scary venture - for the believer and for those who do not believe. It can be intimidating for everyone.

God's way of evangelism always begins with the heart. He desires us to have a heart for the lost but if you find yourself lacking in that department and now wait for a God-given heart attitude toward the lost before you act, consider the story of Jonah. He was called to share the good news to the people of Nineveh. Because of his personal prejudice and disdain for the people, he literally ran from God and from the people that needed to hear. God brought him back to Nineveh after a series of wild events that taught the prophet the lesson of love and forgiveness. When Jonah spoke a word for the people to turn from their sins, the entire city responded and repented. Jonah was bitter because this is exactly what he feared. He even accused God. How sad that Jonah was the reluctant messenger of God's great love, grace and forgiveness.

For us, let's learn the lesson that Jonah so painfully had to find out. It is much better to have a heart attitude that reflects God's heart than to have God discipline us into adopting His heart. He wants us to be broken before Him as we think of the great need in the world and pray and act accordingly. If somehow we find ourselves with a lack in the heart attitude department, may we show honor to God by our actions and let God work on our emotions. It is better to obey God than to wait for emotions to dictate whether we will obey Him or not. Let's speak the good news and call others to repentance whether we feel like it or not. God will honor His word and our actions. We trust He has already been at work in the lives of everyone around us.

When Jonah acted, he had the full assurance he was doing God's will and carried out God's desire. Moses had to pray for assurance in moving the people through the wilderness. He was very careful to honor God and at the proper time, For Moses had said, "If you aren't going with us, don't let us move a step from this place. 16If you don't go with us, who will ever know that I and my people have found favor with you, and that we are different from any other people upon the face of the earth?" (Exodus 33:15) Moses did not want to go ahead of God. During their wandering through the desert, the temptation was to race through the land and makes a quick dash for the promise land. Yet, God led them through the desert at His pace that took them 40 years to complete and a generation to learn the lessons God had to teach. Moses though, recognized the value of getting out of the desert and telling all that God had done for them. Only then would the nations and peoples of the world recognize that their God was the true God and that He had abundantly blessed them.

Today, we need not wait for confirmation from others to tell others about Jesus. It is made abundantly clear! We must tell others. It's only a matter of obediently speaking for God. We tell others for a variety of reasons but the main motivating reason is God's heart — His heart for the lost. This is how we please God! This is good, and pleases God our Savior, who wants all men to be saved and to come to a knowledge of the truth (1 Timothy 2:3-4). If we truly love God and desire to grow, we will want to please Him. If we want to please Him, we will want to adopt His heart. His heart for the lost is an eternal yearning for everyone to return to Him. His heart is broken for the lost. He longs for their return.

Now get this. We are it! God has deemed believers as His sole instrument in the world to reach the lost. If we do not speak about God, people will not hear. "Everyone who calls on the name of the Lord will be saved." How, then, can they call on the one they have not believed in? And how can they believe in the one of whom they have not heard? And how can they hear without someone preaching to them? And how can they preach unless they are sent? (Romans 10:13-15) We've been sent by God Himself. You don't have to wait until you are formally signed up on a mission team to go tell someone about Jesus. When you step out the door today, you are entering the mission field. Enter the world today with God's heart for the lost.

POINT TO PONDER

God wants everyone to be saved.

VERSE TO REMEMBER

Ask of me, and I will make the nations your inheritance,
the ends of the earth your possession.
(Psalm 2:8)

QUESTION TO CONSIDER

Do you love God enough to adopt His desire for the lost?

PRAYER FOCUS

Ask God to use you to bring _____ to Christ.

DAY 15 JOURNAL

_____

_____

_____

Day 16

RECEIVING SEEKERS

> If anyone says, "I love God," yet hates his brother, he is a liar. For anyone who does not love his brother, whom he has seen, cannot love God, whom he has not seen.
>
> (1 John 4:20)

Live with a love for seekers.

Loving those who do not yet know God is like preparing a baby room in your home for the day the newborn will be brought home. Preparations need to be made in order to ensure that the new believer will have a healthy environment which includes a loving family to welcome the new addition to the family.

When does the preparation begin? It begins long before the birth or in this case, spiritual birth. It starts with God's heart that shapes those who follow Him and adopt His heart for the lost. And here is the privilege and also the problem. You see many of us live from Sunday to Sunday when we view our Christian lives. We look at Sunday as the Lord's Day and Monday through Saturday as my days! When we view our lives in such a way, unwholesome attitudes and actions begin to emerge. We can be charming, delightful, accepting, forgiving and just plain loving on Sunday but be a different person altogether during the remainder of the week.

When we get serious about living out a 24/7 Christian life, we begin to evaluate our thoughts, actions and attitudes throughout our day and week. Our words and actions become important not only for our work, family or leisure but because they too are a part of our Christian life. Such a realization helps us evaluate key areas in our lives:

- Heart attitude — do I love God?
- Heart attitude — do I love others as God loves them?
- How can my words reflect God's love towards others?
- How can my actions reflect God's love towards others?
- How can I wisely use my time to bring others closer to God?

- Have I prayed for others around me?

By carefully using opportunities God has for us each day, we are preparing our hearts and others for the day when we will welcome a newborn into the kingdom of God.

Gestation periods are long, laborious but filled with plenty of hope and love. What is the most loving and strategic thing we can do to bring others to Christ? We need to pray for them! 2 Corinthians 4:4 explains, The god of this age has blinded the minds of unbelievers, so that they cannot see the light of the gospel of the glory of Christ, who is the image of God. It's a spiritual issue. Many times when a person does not come to Christ it is not because they do not want to or that they do not understand the words. We need to pray against "spiritual blindness" while God moves and reveals truth in the heart of seekers. You see, it is not people rejecting the message, perhaps it's because the message did not get through in the first place.

How can we be involved in spiritual warfare, and helping others come to Christ?

- Pray for each person by name
- Pray that each person may perceive truth
- Pray that each person may be convicted of sin
- Pray for each person to respond to the prompting of the Holy Spirit
- Pray for each person with perseverance! Don't give up!

POINT TO PONDER

Live with a love for seekers.

VERSE TO REMEMBER

Be very careful, then, how you live — not as unwise but as wise,
making the most of every opportunity.
(Ephesians 5:15-16a)

QUESTION TO CONSIDER

Does my love for God on Sunday show in my love for others during the week?

PRAYER FOCUS

Make a list. Whom do I need to pray will come to Christ?

DAY 16 JOURNAL

Day 17

REACHING OUT TOGETHER

> *Finally, brothers, pray for us that the message of the Lord may spread rapidly and be honored, just as it was with you. And pray that we may be delivered from wicked and evil men, for not everyone has faith. But the Lord is faithful, and he will strengthen and protect you from the evil one.*
> (2 Thessalonians 3:1-3)

We reach out better together.

Very few of us, are super evangelists. God has not gifted the Body of Christ that way. What he has done though is to equip the church with several individuals that can inspire, train and help the greater Body of Christ effectively reach others for Christ. Your small group is such a vehicle. Have you realized that a small group is really a mini-celebration each time you gather? When the fun, fellowship and friendship are flowing, you know that life is good. It's during those times we bask in the goodness of God and sense the flow of God's Spirit. The Body of Christ when it gathers for worship is also a vehicle that demonstrates the full gamut of gifts.

It's also through a group of believers that we can effectively reach others for Christ. Why is that? It's because the Body of Christ is made up of different parts and we make up for each other's deficiencies. Now to each one the manifestation of the Spirit is given for the common good. All these are the work of one and the same Spirit, and he gives them to each one, just as he determines (1 Corinthians 12:7, 11). God knows what is needed in each group. He knows the people around you and the different temperaments and words of wisdom that need to be spoken; as well as acts of kindness that need to be performed. He has placed within each small group individuals with the blend of gifts needed to reach those around you. He also uses you just because you are you. You will reach others because of your life experiences and temperament that others do not.

What are some of the gifts that and skills he uses to bring others to God?

· The inviters

- The sympathizers
- The listeners
- The care givers
- The hospitable
- The encouragers
- The compassionate
- The teachers
- The servers

What we all are responsible to do is found in Romans 12:6-12:

We have different gifts, according to the grace given us. If a man's gift is prophesying, let him use it in proportion to his faith. If it is serving, let him serve; if it is teaching, let him teach; if it is encouraging, let him encourage; if it is contributing to the needs of others, let him give generously; if it is leadership, let him govern diligently; if it is showing mercy, let him do it cheerfully. Love must be sincere. Hate what is evil; cling to what is good. Be devoted to one another in brotherly love. Honor one another above yourselves. Never be lacking in zeal, but keep your spiritual fervor, serving the Lord. Be joyful in hope, patient in affliction, faithful in prayer.

- Love others
- Devoted to each other
- Passionate for God
- Joyful in hope
- Patient in affliction
- Faithful in prayer

You might say the above list cuts across spiritual gifts and callings. It is a solid list of what each and every Christian needs to be involved with. No matter what gift we have been given to serve God and others, we are to faithfully continue in prayer! We can each pray and we need to pray together. There is power when we pray together. When we name people God has placed on our hearts and we bring them before others, spiritual power comes when we agree in the Name of God. The power of God comes when we agree in prayer:

"I tell you the truth, whatever you bind on earth will be bound in heaven, and whatever you loose on earth will be loosed in heaven. "Again, I tell you that if two of you on earth agree about anything you ask for, it will be done for you by my Father in heaven. For where two or three come together in my name, there am I with them."
(Matthew 18:18-20)

God has given the church — authority! This is powerful. We may not realize the immense power He has given over to the church. When we pray together, we set in motion God's power to reach people for Christ. But not so fast. Before God answers our prayer, there is an issue of unity! He doesn't want us to just come together; He wants our spirits to "agree." The word "agree" means "to stand together." God doesn't just want us together in the same room; He wants us to be shoulder to shoulder, hearts and minds united by the Spirit of God. Our hearts must be aligned and our minds singular. In a word, unity! You see, one Christian praying is powerful but when you get 2 or 3 or 50 or 1000 together, the power is multiplied — all focused on the same need!

POINT TO PONDER

We reach out better together.

VERSE TO REMEMBER

For where two or three come together in my name, there am I with them. (Matthew 18:20)

QUESTION TO CONSIDER

Have you experienced the exponential power of corporate prayer?

PRAYER FOCUS

Maximize your prayer effectiveness by praying frequently with others.

DAY 17 JOURNAL

_____

_____

_____

_____

_____

_____

_____

_____

Day 18

REACHING OUT THROUGH FELT NEEDS

> *Because he himself suffered when he was tempted, he is able to help those who are being tempted.*
> (Hebrews 2:18)

Meeting felt needs lead to spiritual openness.

Everyone has them. They may be softened through time, forgotten long ago, or kept alive daily only to wound us again. Hurts. Everyone has them. It may be as big as a loss of a loved one, the break up of a relationship, personal illness or it can be as small as getting a traffic ticket, stubbing your toe, or missing an appointment. But nonetheless, life produces hurts. Any hurt or any area of need a person experiences is a felt need.

Everyone has them. The people around us may seem they have life under control but hurts will come. When they encounter hurts, we have an opportunity to reach out to them. Hurts are opportunities for ministry. Some hurts are easy to solve or get over. Other hurts require a lot more attention. Some hurts may not be the greatest needs in life but they do open the door for us to show God is cares for them and so do we.

Have you ever noticed you have a particular soft spot in your heart for people who have gone through similar hurts you have previously experienced? This is not an accident. God placed hurts and experiences in your life so that in the future you will be able to help others.

> *Praise be to the God and Father of our Lord Jesus Christ, the Father of compassion and the God of all comfort, who comforts us in all our troubles, so that we can comfort those in any trouble with the comfort we ourselves have received from God. For just as the sufferings of Christ flow over into our lives, so also through Christ our comfort overflows. If we are distressed, it is for your comfort and salvation; if we are comforted, it is for your comfort, which produces in you patient endurance of the same sufferings we suffer.*
> (2 Corinthians 1:3-6)

God allowed difficult experiences in your life to grow and mature you. Life experiences become powerful tools in our lives since we can readily identify with the dilemmas, demands and decisions that need to be made. Sure we could keep it to ourselves but God has a far more reaching plan for you. He wants you to use your experiences to help others through their difficulties.

What gives us the assurance to help others in need? First, we must recognize that any "comfort" that we can share with others, we first received from God. At the right time, we are able to pass it on. Second, we direct them to Jesus who fully understands them. Because he himself suffered when he was tempted, he is able to help those who are being tempted (Hebrews 2:18). Thirdly, we can let people know, whatever they are going through, there is a way out. No temptation has seized you except what is common to man. And God is faithful; he will not let you be tempted beyond what you can bear. But when you are tempted, he will also provide a way out so that you can stand up under it (1 Corinthians 10:13).

The Apostle Paul lived a life devoted to God and with a heart to reach the lost. Therefore I endure everything for the sake of the elect, that they too may obtain the salvation that is in Christ Jesus, with eternal glory (2 Timothy 2:10). Knowing God works through us and even commissions us to help others, how can we minister through felt needs?

- Pray for sensitivity. If we don't recognize the difficulties others are facing, we will not be much help to them. A great deal to sensitivity is letting the other person speak — be a good listener.
- Pray for what to say.
  Nothing is more encouraging than a timely word; A word aptly spoken is like apples of gold in settings of silver. (Proverbs 25:11)
- Pray we can empathize with them.
  Praise be to the God and Father of our Lord Jesus Christ, the Father of compassion and the God of all comfort, who comforts us in all our troubles, so that we can comfort those in any trouble with the comfort we ourselves have received from God.
  (2 Corinthians 1:3-4)
- Pray for them and with them.
  Therefore he is able to save completely those who come to God through him, because he always lives to intercede for them. (Hebrews 7:25)
- Meet their need. If it is within your means, pray how God can use you. Do they have material needs? Do they need emotional support? Do they need a friend? Do they need someone to spend time with them? Do they need guidance toward eternal answers?

By letting God know you are available to help those in need, He will direct you to those you are uniquely made to help.

POINT TO PONDER

Meeting felt needs leads to spiritual openness.

VERSE TO REMEMBER

Praise be to the God and Father of our Lord Jesus Christ, the Father of compassion and the God of all comfort, who comforts us in all our troubles, so that we can comfort those in any trouble with the comfort we ourselves have received from God.
(2 Corinthians 1:3-4)

QUESTION TO CONSIDER

When others express their needs to you, are you available to help?

PRAYER FOCUS

Develop sensitivity in your spirit so God can easily direct you.

DAY 18 JOURNAL

_____

_____

_____

_____

_____

_____

_____

_____

_____

_____

_____

_____

Day 19

REACHING OUT THROUGH GENUINE FRIENDSHIP

> *Be wise in the way you act toward outsiders; make the most of every opportunity.*
> *Let your conversation be always full of grace, seasoned with salt,*
> *so that you may know how to answer everyone.*
> (Colossians 4:5-6)

Friends tell friends what is most important.

Friends care deeply about one another. We have friends that are casual acquaintances, coworkers, classmates, and people we run across in our business. A special class of people, our friends, is the ones we confide in and share what is important. However, we need not reserve what is most important in our lives to those closest to us. Our faith is too important not to share! Yet, we usually don't go grabbing the first person on the street corner and set him down. God uses our relationships with others to reach them. It comes from earning the right to speak.

This is so important the Apostle Paul would go to any extreme, without sacrificing and honoring God, to win people for the Lord. To the weak I became weak, to win the weak. I have become all things to all men so that by all possible means I might save some (1 Corinthians 9:22). He had to spend time away from his closest friends, family and other believers in order to win others to God. He made a conscious decision to make new friends for the cause of Christ. In essence, the Apostle Paul loved people without first knowing them. He adopted God's heart for the lost.

The Apostle Paul genuinely loved people and reached out because he cared for them and their eternal destiny. His pattern for living set in motion the outreach of the early church and reaches us even today. He was solid, conservative in his beliefs but radical, liberal in his practice. He went out of the box; literally, he left the temples of his day and brought it out to the streets, overseas and wherever God would take him.

In Colossians 4:5-6, He tells us how to reach people for Christ:

- *Be wise in the way you act.* How you begin the day with God, your spiritual temperature for the day and your spiritual condition will come out in your interactions with others. Prepare yourself early in heart, spirit and soul preparation before God. Then you will be able to live a life that will glorify God. They want so see God's control in your life. They want to see the character of Christ shining through. It's impossible when we are relying on the flesh and the ugliness of the sinful nature comes out. So, pray up and be wise in how you act.
- *Make the most of every opportunity.* Opportunities abound with each interaction you have with people. Pray for God's Spirit to give you sensitivity to timing, wording and actions. Some things you can prepare in advance and others God reveals to you at that moment. Here are some of the things you can do in advance: write out your testimony, emphasizing the work of God in your life; learn the basic principles of the gospel and practice it until you know it by heart; decide daily, before stepping out of your door that you will respond when God opens your eyes to opportunities to serve others.
- *Let your conversation be always full of grace, seasoned with salt.* Learn to be a graceful speaker. No, it doesn't meet you will need to be a world class orator before God can use you. It means that you add the grace of God not only in your beliefs but in your speech. Speak with love on your lips; don't judge others. Use words that encourage or are helpful. Salt is a preservative that makes food last longer; it also gives it flavor. May your speech be prolonged because people like talking to you and you add flavor to conversation. When this happens, you know your speech has been seasoned with the love and grace of God.
- *So that you may know how to answer everyone.* Now this seems like it is impossible, and it is within our own strength. That is why God invites us to ask Him for wisdom, the first step in this process, If any of you lacks wisdom, he should ask God, who gives generously to all without finding fault, and it will be given to him (James 1:5). I love that! He doesn't find fault with us not knowing. He simply tells us to ask and it will be given. You will receive the wisdom to answer everyone with grace and love.

POINT TO PONDER

Friends tell friends what is most important.

VERSE TO REMEMBER

Be wise in the way you act toward outsiders; make the most of every
opportunity. Let your conversation be always full of grace, seasoned with salt,
so that you may know how to answer everyone.
(Colossians 4:5-6)

QUESTION TO CONSIDER

Are you a good friend?

PRAYER FOCUS

In order to be heard by man, begin in prayer to God.

DAY 19 JOURNAL

_____

_____

_____

_____

_____

_____

_____

_____

_____

_____

_____

_____

_____

_____

_____

_____

_____

_____

_____

Day 20

REACHING OUT THROUGH ACTIONS

> *And do not forget to do good and to share with others, for with such sacrifices God is pleased.*
> (Hebrews 13:16)

Actions show people we care.

Actions are the proof of our love for others. Words without action is like clouds without rain; an empty promise without fulfillment. We need words of love and acts of love to back them up. As the body without the spirit is dead, so faith without deeds is dead (James 2:26). Actions are an extension of the goodness of God in our lives. When God called us to Himself, He also sent us out into the world. Reaching out to others is a response to following Jesus.

Jesus taught, an act of love can be as small as providing a cup of water. And if anyone gives even a cup of cold water to one of these little ones because he is my disciple, I tell you the truth, he will certainly not lose his reward (Matthew 14:42). In fact, he has acts of kindness for you to do each day. For we are God's workmanship, created in Christ Jesus to do good works, which God prepared in advance for us to do (Ephesians 2:10).

It was so important for Jesus to receive instruction from God the Father that He prayed constantly. For the Father loves the Son and shows him all he does. Yes, to your amazement he will show him even greater things than these (John 5:20). He relied on God the Father through the Holy Spirit while He was on earth. More importantly, Jesus' motive for reaching out was to please the Father. By myself I can do nothing; I judge only as I hear, and my judgment is just, for I seek not to please myself but him who sent me (John 5:30). Only as the Father instructed Him did Jesus act. Jesus' love for the people was not only in his heart but needed to be demonstrated, ultimately on the cross..

Your motive for actions must also be to please the Lord. If it is to please others, you will be disappointed. You may even find yourself unappreciated such as those that Saint Peter wrote to, Live such good lives among the pagans that, though they accuse you of doing wrong, they may see your good deeds and glorify God on the day he visits us (1 Peter 2:12). Yet, whether in eternity or now in God's eyes, if you keep pleasing God as your main motive, you will know the joy of serving God whether others appreciate your actions or not. You will be free to seek God, serve God, and serve others when you know your service is for the Lord.

How can you prepare to be used of God?

· Spend time with God.
· Ask God to prompt you to action.
· As God reveals needs, pray for your involvement.
· Intentionally decide to take appropriate action.

When you do take action, make sure it is practical. Help with laundry, take out the garbage, baby-sit for a couple, provide meals during a hectic time, provide transportation, or even a cup of water. The possibilities are endless as God directs you to specific action. Since God is your motive to serve, with others around you as the recipients, you are free from the expectation that they need to return your favor. You act out of obedience to what God wants. If you love me, you will obey what I command (John 14:15). What a freeing feeling, knowing serving others is part of your service to God.

We have received much so much is required of us. Now it is required that those who have been given a trust must prove faithful (1 Corinthians 4:2).

POINT TO PONDER

Actions show people we care.

VERSE TO REMEMBER

For we are God's workmanship, created in Christ Jesus to do good works, which God prepared in advance for us to do.
(Ephesians 2:10)

QUESTION TO CONSIDER

What good works is God prompting you to do?

PRAYER FOCUS

Meet with God often to hear what God is saying you ought to do.

DAY 20 JOURNAL

Day 21

REACHING OUT THROUGH VERBAL WITNESS

> *Yet when I preach the gospel, I cannot boast, for I am compelled to preach.*
> *Woe to me if I do not preach the gospel!*
> (1 Corinthians 9:16)

We can't help but tell others the Good News.

Telling others the Good News of Jesus Christ is intricately tied to our relationship with God and with others. When you have something good to tell you cannot help but shout it out. It may be a present, a promotion, or a passion but they all have the same effect on you — you can't help but tell others. It's the same with the love of God. The Apostle Paul felt the Good News so deeply that he said he was "compelled to preach." He couldn't hold back.

In fact, he felt he was commissioned of God speak to others. As an ambassador he could not wait to tell as many as possible in his lifetime. He implored them to come and respond to God's invitation. We are therefore Christ's ambassadors, as though God were making his appeal through us. We implore you on Christ's behalf: Be reconciled to God. God made him who had no sin to be sin for us, so that in him we might become the righteousness of God (2 Corinthians 5:20-21). His pleadings were emotion-filled but also full of reason and illustrations.

Yet, the Apostle Paul was aware of his own failings. He did not dare rely on himself. He asked others to pray for him so that he would have the words to speak, Pray also for me, that whenever I open my mouth, words may be given me so that I will fearlessly make known the mystery of the gospel (Ephesians 6:19). He also asked for prayer so that he may speak clearly, Pray that I may proclaim it clearly, as I should (Colossians 4:4). Personal commitment, trying harder and working out a better plan just doesn't cut it in the spiritual world. It takes God's hand, on God's vessels to accomplish God's work.

He realized doors of opportunity were not in his power. He prayed that God would open those doors, In my prayers at all times; and I pray that now at last by God's will the way may be opened for me to come to you (Romans

1:10). Our responsibility is to take the opportunities when they come. Speak clearly and with conviction regarding the Good News. Through Jesus we can introduce people to God.

And in this one body to reconcile both of them to God through the cross, by which he put to death their hostility. He came and preached peace to you who were far away and peace to those who were near. For through him we both have access to the Father by one Spirit.

(Ephesians 2:16-18)

What can you do today to bring others to faith?

- Pray for them consistently.
  Prayer breaks down spiritual barriers in order for them to comprehend.
- Pray for God to use you as His spokesperson.
  Pray that God will use your words and actions to lead others to Him.
- Express your concern personally.
  Keep it personal. Share how God cares for each of them.
- Express your concern regarding their spiritual condition.
  Some people may never have thought of their spiritual well-being.
- Express your own testimony.
  Share how you came to Christ and what you appreciate about God.
- Express God's grace, love, and forgiveness are available to them today.
  Move the Good News from history, to your story to His (Jesus) story, to finally make it their story.
- Lead them in prayer to receive Jesus
  Prayer is a conversation between a person and God.
  Help your friend address God directly.

POINT TO PONDER

We can't help but tell others the Good News.

VERSE TO REMEMBER

I pray that you may be active in sharing your faith, so that you will have a full understanding of every good thing we have in Christ. (Philemon 1:6)

QUESTION TO CONSIDER

Will anyone hear the Good News spoken by you this week?

PRAYER FOCUS

When God opens doors of opportunity, may you use them to speak for Christ.

DAY 21 JOURNAL

_____

_____

_____

_____

_____

_____

_____

_____

_____

_____

_____

_____

_____

_____

_____

_____

_____

_____

_____

Pray for Mutual Encouragement

Day 22

UNIFYING ONE ANOTHER

> *Father, just as you are in me and I am in you. May they also be in us so that the world may believe that you have sent me. I have given them the glory that you gave me, that they may be one as we are one: I in them and you in me. May they be brought to complete unity to let the world know that you sent me and have loved them even as you have loved me.*
>
> (John 17:21-23)

Unity in the Spirit is the basis of our fellowship.

One of the most remarkable traits of Jesus' disciples and of the early church was the high level of diversity yet the strength of unity among them. They were from different ethnic, regional, political and socio-economic groups yet they remained united. The secret was in their God Himself that united the people. Certainly if they concentrated on their differences, divisions and flair ups would have been common place.

Some people wait until they find people "just like them" before they include them in their inner circle. Needless to say, they do not find many. No, those with rich and growing relationships recognize differences, even celebrate those differences but find their strength and commonality in Christ. So, unity is not the absence of differences but the product of lives given to God. When we submit our lives to God, we're perfectly at home with others who have done the same — God is the great Unifier.

Read God's heart concerning unity, How good and pleasant it is when brothers live together in unity! (Psalm 133:1). God wants us to pursue it, keep it and guard it. God is not content with us having positional unity, which is our standing as brothers and sisters in Christ, without its practice. Jesus knew this was so crucial, he prayed for unity in his High Priestly Prayer, I in them and you in me. May they be brought to complete unity to let the world know that you sent me and have loved them even as you have loved me (John 17:23).

How will the world know about our unity in Jesus if we do not live it out? Our unity must be put into practice. St. Peter gives us ample instruction on how to live out our unity, Finally, all of you, live in harmony with one another; be sympathetic, love as brothers, be compassionate and humble. Do not repay evil with evil or insult with insult, but with blessing, because to this you were called so that you may inherit a blessing. For, "Whoever would love life and see good days must keep his tongue from evil and his lips from deceitful speech. He must turn from evil and do good; he must seek peace and pursue it. For the eyes of the Lord are on the righteous and his ears are attentive to their prayer, but the face of the Lord is against those who do evil." (1 Peter 3:8-12). He is saying, if we are in Christ, don't just say it — you must put it into practice. Don't rest on the fact that you have Jesus but you treat others badly. On the contrary, since you have Jesus in your life, you need to live out the inward reality.

Here are some ways that may help:

- As you get up each day, submit your heart to God's leading.
- Watch what you say — and how you say it.
- Don't play "Devil's advocate" — why stick up for the Devil?! When possible, be agreeable.
- Be considerate, compassionate and commendable — strive for goodness.
- Be a people uniter, not a people separator.
- Pray together often.

It's true, "the family that prays together stays together." It's also true for friends, small groups, churches, and nations. God desires to bring everyone to Him (the Great Uniter); it is Satan that wants to divide. You can be used of God today to bring others together. Why not adopt St. Paul's prayer for yourself today? May the God who gives endurance and encouragement give you a spirit of unity among yourselves as you follow Christ Jesus (Romans 15:5).

POINT TO PONDER

Unity in the Spirit is the basis of our fellowship.

VERSE TO REMEMBER

Make every effort to keep the unity of the Spirit through the bond of peace. (Ephesians 4:3)

QUESTION TO CONSIDER

What can you do to unify the people you will interact with in the next 24 hours?

PRAYER FOCUS

Pray God will make you a uniter and not a separator.

DAY 22 JOURNAL

_____

_____

_____

_____

_____

_____

_____

_____

_____

_____

_____

_____

_____

_____

_____

_____

_____

_____

_____

_____

_____

_____

_____

_____

Day 23

LOVING ONE ANOTHER

Love must be sincere. Hate what is evil; cling to what is good. Be devoted to one another in brotherly love. Honor one another above yourselves. Never be lacking in zeal, but keep your spiritual fervor, serving the Lord.
(Romans 12:9-11)

You only love to the extent you show it.

Be a great lover! The capacity you have to love will determine how much God can use you. The more God has a hold of you, the more of the Fruit of the Spirit, the main fruit being love, you will show in your life. You see, some people are mean not because they choose to be mean but they don't have any capacity to love; or their capacity to love is so small, it is hardly felt by others. Our goal is for God to have complete control over us so that His nature, love, can shine forth.

Loving others, the second greatest commandment is an overflow of the greatest command, to love God. "Teacher, which is the greatest commandment in the Law?" Jesus replied: "'Love the Lord your God with all your heart and with all your soul and with all your mind.' this is the first and greatest commandment. And the second is like it: 'Love your neighbor as yourself.' All the Law and the Prophets hang on these two commandments" (Matthew 22:36-40). Another way to put it is, to the extent we love others is the true extent that we love God!

Where do we start? It begins with your heart condition. God desires your heart and so does everyone else. Nothing is worse than to go through life without your heart being engaged. Real living begins when hearts are engaged with the Spirit of God. Then, God works through us to touch the lives of everyone that crosses our path. It is Christ's love flowing through us. This was also the Apostle Paul's prayer for the believers around him, I pray that out of his glorious riches he may strengthen you with power through his Spirit in your inner being (Ephesians 3:16). The strengthening power of the Holy Spirit grips our lives and moves us from ordinary living to spirit-filled vessels for His use.

In essence, we need heart transformations; this is the revival needed today. It's not more knowledge, programs or gimmicks. The needful step of loving and yielding to God leads to an inner transformation that allows God to work freely through us. It's quite a sight to see one person walking in the power of the Holy Spirit; but imagine a whole congregation, community or country following hard after God!

Love is not something soft but is extremely strong. Yet it must be guarded, nurtured and cherished. Time after time, Jesus, the Apostle Paul, Peter and others in the early church warned against growing cold in their love for God and others. Jesus warned, Because of the increase of wickedness, the love of most will grow cold (Matthew 24:12). Jesus spoke these words in relation to the end times and the "spirit of the age". Love goes against the tide and the norm of our culture and aims higher than self-preservation; the love of God and others.

What steps can we take to love others? The steps are summarized in Jesus' answer to what are the two greatest commandments:

- Love God and yield to His ways.
- Love people with the love of God.

Where this becomes extremely practical is in the home, where the people closest to you see you. Here's how St. Peter saw love working in the family, Wives, submit to your husbands, as is fitting in the Lord. Husbands, love your wives and do not be harsh with them (Colossians 3:18). Also, Husbands, in the same way be considerate as you live with your wives, and treat them with respect as the weaker partner and as heirs with you of the gracious gift of life, so that nothing will hinder your prayers (1 Peter 3:7). Notice for husbands, an added incentive to treat our wives well includes unhindered prayers! God has set it up so we need to constantly nurture our key relationships or our prayers will not be effective.

It's as if God is saying if you don't love key people in your life — God, and family, how can you learn to love others? When you are controlled by God, the essence of His character will fill your life. Love will exude from you because you are "controlled by God's Spirit." The most famous chapter in the Bible on love, 1 Corinthians 13, is essentially a description of love in action. When you see or sense these traits, you know someone is showing love. You know someone is controlled by God.

Love is patient, love is kind. It does not envy, it does not boast, it is not proud.
It is not rude, it is not self-seeking, it is not easily angered, it keeps no record of wrongs.
Love does not delight in evil but rejoices with the truth. It always protects, always trusts,
always hopes, always perseveres.

Love never fails.
(1 Corinthians 13:4-8)

Look at the clear connection between a life controlled by God and a life of love:

The end of all things is near. Therefore be clear minded and self-controlled so that you can pray. Above all, love each other deeply, because love covers over a multitude of sins.
(1 Peter 4:7-8)

POINT TO PONDER

You only love to the extent you show it.

VERSE TO REMEMBER

The end of all things is near. Therefore be clear minded and self-controlled so that you can pray. Above all, love each other deeply, because love covers over a multitude of sins.
(1 Peter 4:7-8)

QUESTION TO CONSIDER

Do others know you love them through your actions?

PRAYER FOCUS

How much you love others is the true indicator of how much you love God.

DAY 23 JOURNAL

_____

_____

_____

_____

_____

_____

_____

Day 24

SUBMITTING TO ONE ANOTHER

> *Submit to one another out of reverence for Christ.*
> (Ephesians 5:21)

Submission lifts others without minimizing self.

Submission should be a given. Webster's Dictionary defines "submission" as, "To give in to the authority, power, or desires of another." Submission recognizes those who have authority over us. A child learns from an early age that parents have authority over him; a student learns a teacher has authority over her; and as employees we recognize bosses have authority over us. And ultimately, all of us need to be in submission to God because He is our ultimate authority. Look at the authorities that God says we need to submit to:

- Government
  Everyone must submit himself to the governing authorities, for there is no authority except that which God has established. The authorities that exist have been established by God. (Romans 13:1)
- Leaders
  Obey your leaders and submit to their authority. They keep watch over you as men who must give an account. Obey them so that their work will be a joy, not a burden, for that would be of no advantage to you. (Hebrews 13:17)
- Bosses
  Slaves, submit yourselves to your masters with all respect, not only to those who are good and considerate, but also to those who are harsh. (1 Peter 2:18)
- Husbands and wives
  Also for husbands and wives, Submit to one another out of reverence for Christ. Wives, submit to your husbands as to the Lord. For the husband is the head of the wife as Christ is the head of the church, his body, of which he is the Savior. Now as the church submits to Christ, so also wives should submit to their husbands in everything. Husbands, love your wives, just as Christ loved the church and gave himself up for her. (Ephesians 5:21-25)
- Parents
  Children, obey your parents in everything, for this pleases the Lord. (Colossians 3:20)

·   God

Do not be stiff-necked, as your fathers were; submit to the LORD. (2 Chronicles 30:8)
Submit yourselves, then, to God. Resist the devil, and he will flee from you. (James 4:7)
*Even Jesus Himself submitted Himself fully to God the Father, During the days of Jesus'
life on earth, he offered up prayers and petitions with loud cries and tears to the one
who could save him from death, and he was heard because of his reverent submission.*
(Hebrews 5:7)

Why is submission such an important topic in Scripture? Rebellion, the
opposite of submission, is the worst possible sin condition. For rebellion is like
the sin of divination, and arrogance like the evil of idolatry (1 Samuel 15:23).
Satan even caused David to sin against God, Satan rose up against Israel and
incited David to take a census of Israel (1 Chronicles 21:1). To rebel against
God's authority is the same as idolatry, setting up another source in the place
of God! God will deal severely with rebellion, An evil man is bent only on
rebellion; a merciless official will be sent against him (Proverbs 17:11).

When we submit to the authorities God has placed over us, we are
indirectly submitting to God's authority. If authorities become evil though, God
can remove them. In the meanwhile, we are to submit to their authority. Take
parents for instance. Parents have authority over their children. Certainly no
parent today would claim perfection. Yet, a child cannot use this as an excuse
not to obey. We please God when we follow those God has placed in authority
over us.

As believers, we are called to submit to one another. It's not a matter of
rank but of deference to one another. When we submit to one another, we are
following God's example and command. How does this work? What does it
look like?

·   Don't insist on your opinion; hold your preferences lightly
·   Serve others by responding to their preferences
·   Have an attitude of

POINT TO PONDER

Submission lifts others without minimizing self.

VERSE TO REMEMBER

Submit to one another out of reverence for Christ.
(Ephesians 5:21)

QUESTION TO CONSIDER

Do you live a life that indicates you are under authority or do others believe you are an authority unto yourself?

PRAYER FOCUS

Submission strengthens your standing with God and others.

DAY 24 JOURNAL

_____

_____

_____

_____

_____

_____

_____

_____

_____

_____

_____

_____

_____

_____

_____

_____

_____

_____

_____

_____

Day 25

FORGIVING ONE ANOTHER

> *Bear with each other and forgive whatever grievances you may have against one another.*
> *Forgive as the Lord forgave you.*
> (Colossians 3:13)

Forgiveness allows both parties to walk in freedom.

Forgiveness is the common practice between people when we realize we are all imperfect. If we start here, admitting our collective shortcomings, the world would be a place. God instructs us to forgive each other and to do it quickly. "If he sins against you seven times in a day, and seven times comes back to you and says, 'I repent,' forgive him." (Luke 17:4). We need to follow Christ's example, Jesus said, "Father, forgive them, for they do not know what they are doing" (Luke 23:34). When wrongfully crucified, Jesus prayed for those responsible and asked God to forgive them. For us not to forgive would go against Christ's command and example.

When we realize the enormous amount, an eternity's worth of punishment Jesus took on our behalf, we see the offenses against us are minute in comparison. In fact, Jesus told the parable of a king and his servant. The servant owed him a very large sum of money. So much that it was clear he would not be able to repay it even if it took him the rest of his life. The king forgave him his debt but the servant went out and demanded repayment from a friend who only owed him a few dollars. Notice the indignation of the king towards the servant who refused to forgive, Then the master called the servant in. 'You wicked servant,' he said, 'I canceled all that debt of yours because you begged me to. Shouldn't you have had mercy on your fellow servant just as I had on you?' (Matthew 18:32-33).

We must forgive since God forgave us. Get rid of all bitterness, rage and anger, brawling and slander, along with every form of malice. Be kind and compassionate to one another, forgiving each other, just as in Christ God forgave you (Ephesians 4:31-32). It's so important to God He says we shouldn't even continue to worship until we have forgiven. "Therefore, if you are offering your gift at the altar and there remember that your brother has something against you, leave your gift there in front of the altar. First go and be reconciled to your brother; then come and offer your gift (Matthew 5:23-24).

We tend to see forgiveness as letting the other guy off the hook. Actually, we have much to benefit when we forgive others. And when you stand praying, if you hold anything against anyone, forgive him, so that your Father in heaven may forgive you your sins. (Mark 11:25-26) Now, this is not a matter of salvation but of fellowship. If we do not forgive wrongs committed against us, the sins and the consequences remain; they are not forgiven. When we do forgive, they are removed; the curse is lifted and fellowship can be restored.

This is not life or death but close. Forgiveness allows the other person to walk free and us as well. If you forgive anyone his sins, they are forgiven; if you do not forgive them, they are not forgiven. (John 20:23)

When we do not forgive, or let them go, we suffer the most since we need to keep a vigilant watch lest our captive escape. It takes a lot of emotional energy not to forgive. To make matters worse, the other person may not even be aware of our unforgiveness!

Look at God's readiness to forgive when we go to Him, If we confess our sins, he is faithful and just and will forgive us our sins and purify us from all unrighteousness (1 John 1:9). Only as we pray and allow God to transform us will we do what is natural in the kingdom — forgive.

POINT TO PONDER

Forgiveness allows both parties to walk in freedom.

VERSE TO REMEMBER

From the Lord's Prayer:
Forgive us our debts, as we also have forgiven our debtors
(Matthew 6:12)

QUESTION TO CONSIDER

Are you busy playing prison guard?
If so, who do you need to let go, forgive, today?

PRAYER FOCUS

Forgive everyone that God brings to your mind.

DAY 25 JOURNAL

Day 26

HONORING ONE ANOTHER

> *He will turn the hearts of the fathers to their children,*
> *and the hearts of the children to their fathers.*
> (Malachi 4:6a)

When we honor others we honor God.

Honor, or high respect, is a gift we give to others. It begins with God and spreads to others. God calls us to honor Him by honoring others. From God, we learn to honor Him and those around us. O LORD, our God, other lords besides you have ruled over us, but your name alone do we honor (Isaiah 26:13). Everything good comes from God and is an extension of His goodness. When we honor God, we gain His heart for His creation. So God created man in his own image, in the image of God he created him; male and female he created them (Genesis 1:27).

Each person is a special creation of God and deserves honor. Show proper respect to everyone (1 Peter 2:17). We will even come to the place to demonstrate special honor those who are weaker. On the contrary, those parts of the body that seem to be weaker are indispensable, and the parts that we think are less honorable we treat with special honor (1 Corinthians 12:22-23). Everyone then, whether in high respectable positions or lowly, unseemly positions are to be honored. Honor given to others is a response to God's creation.

When we honor others, we do not judge them because they are poor or rich; old or young; skilled or clumsy; black or white; or any other category that superficially divides people. We honor them because they are created in the image of God. They are special in God's eyes. Only those who have adopted God's heart can see through God's eyes. It takes prayer; it takes a heart relationship with God that changes our attitudes and perceptions of others.

When we do this, we won't have to worry about our own honor. God promises to do the exalting. The reward of humility and the fear of the LORD are riches, honor, and life (Proverbs 22:4). If we humble ourselves and respond to God, he will honor us in due time. How do we honor God?

- When we do God's work.
  If anyone serves Me, the Father will honor him. (John 12:26)
- When we humble ourselves.
  Everyone who exalts himself will be humbled, and he who humbles himself will be exalted.
  (Luke 14:11)

We can take active steps when we take steps to obey God; and to humble ourselves.

How can we honor others?

- Honor others by giving them our attention
- Honor others by complimenting them
- Honor others by recognizing their accomplishments
- Honor others by celebrating their uniqueness
- Honor others by being humble
- Honor others by valuing them
- Honor others by spending time with them
- Honor others by praying for them

When you do this, you begin to value people and love them as God loves them.

It begins with you and those closest to you. Honor your father and your mother, so that you may live long in the land the Lord your God is giving you. (Exodus 20:12). Also fathers toward their children, Fathers, do not exasperate your children; instead, bring them up in the training and instruction of the Lord (Ephesians 6:4). No wonder family lines are blessed when we follow God. In humility and honor, God promises to bless families that love him a thousand generations.

> *You shall not bow down to them (false idols) or worship them; for I,*
> *the LORD your God, am a jealous God, punishing the children for the sin of the fathers*
> *to the third and fourth generation of those who hate me, but showing love to*
> *a thousand generations of those who love me and keep my commandments.*
> (Deuteronomy 5:9-10)

POINT TO PONDER

When we honor others we honor God.

VERSE TO REMEMBER

Honor one another above yourselves.
(Romans 12:10)

QUESTION TO CONSIDER

Has your love for God overflowed to the point of honoring others?

PRAYER FOCUS

God, open my eyes to see the value of each individual you bring into my life.

DAY 26 JOURNAL

_____

_____

_____

_____

_____

_____

_____

_____

_____

_____

_____

_____

_____

_____

_____

_____

_____

Day 27

LISTENING TO ONE ANOTHER

> *Everyone should be quick to listen.*
> (James 1:19a)

Listen because God speaks through others.

God made the Body of Believers to work together. When we listen to others, we acknowledge God is active and speaking through ordinary people. God even spoke through a donkey to reach hardheaded Balaam (see Numbers 22:28-30); certainly He will speak through others who have the Spirit of God dwelling in them. When we listen, we are in a posture to learn, display honor and humility.

Listening is a gift to others. Listening is more than silence; it is active engagement of our minds and hearts. When we listen we give the very best we have — we give our attention, time and self to others. To do this, we must be sensitive to what God is saying through others. How can we tune in to God's wavelength?

Preparation, the time before we interact with anyone else is the key. Our time with God prepares us to meet others. When in the company of dignitaries or others we esteem, we tend to ask questions and desire to hear what they say. In God's presence, we wait for Him to speak and learn to hear what He is saying. We do not impose our agenda on God but rather wait for Him to speak.

In His presence, we become aware of our own failings and lack of perfection. We learn to seek God for His grace each day. When we start the day on our knees, a posture of humility, we learn patience and value what God says to us. When we spend time listening to God, we train ourselves to listen by the Spirit of God, to tune in with what He is saying through others.

How can we be better listeners?

- We listen to people when we focus with our eyes, heart and mind. People want to know we are tracking with them when they speak. Make contact with those you are speaking and pray for sensitivity, not only in the words spoken but also in attitudes.

· We listen to people when we give them permission to continue. Throughout our day, people drop small comments looking for others who are truly interested in their well-being. Take for example, the typical greeting, "Hi, how are you?" The normal response is, "Fine, thank you" or "Alright, how are you?" But before the person begins to tell us more, we've already walked by. Our potential question that carries promise of a caring soul turns into no more than a formal greeting. Stop long enough to go beneath the surface. Allow them tell their story.

· We listen to people when we respond with proper emotions. Rejoice with those who rejoice; mourn with those who mourn (Romans 12:15). How insensitive it would be for us to not identify with a person's emotions when they are sharing. On the other hand, how affirming it is when we have found one who has given of their time and emotion, communicating they care through their listening.

· We listen to people when we respond by praying for them. If we have understood what has been said, we can pray for God to do a work in the person's life. If good news has been shared, we can thank God and pray for continued blessing. If a need is presented, especially if the person is in need of direction, we can pray for God's wisdom. As a guideline, when a request is communicated, if we have listened, we will pray to God, the One who is truly eager to hear.

POINT TO PONDER

Listen because God speaks through others.

VERSE TO REMEMBER

Let the wise listen and add to their learning,
and let the discerning get guidance.
(Proverbs 1:5)

QUESTION TO CONSIDER

How spiritually ready are you to listen to others?

PRAYER FOCUS

Spend time with God is the best preparation to hear others.

DAY 27 JOURNAL

Day 28

PRAYING FOR ONE ANOTHER

> *And pray in the Spirit on all occasions with all kinds of prayers and requests.*
> *With this in mind, be alert and always keep on praying for all the saints.*
> (Ephesians 6:18)

Our immediate response towards others is to pray.

We need to pray together and we need to pray for each other. The power of God is available to us when we pray. Sharing and discussion informs but does not bring the power of God to bear. Only when we bring our requests to God in united in prayer, does God act. Why? When we pray together it is our declaration of dependence upon Him.

We sometimes get hung up between individual prayer and corporate prayer. Both are essential. Sometimes individual prayer is used an excuse not to pray together. What we really need is a biblical understanding. The classic passage for individual prayer is found in Matthew 6:6, But when you pray, go into your room, close the door and pray to your Father, who is unseen. Then your Father, who sees what is done in secret, will reward you. When we read this we might imagine our own little 2 x 3 foot closet where we have our little mag light as we quietly read the Scriptures and pray. We need a better understanding. The "closet" was actually a room for dignitaries much like a living room where guests were welcomed. It was a much more public place. In fact, Matthew 6 stresses the need to pray together, corporately and with humility.

God brings situations into our lives to teach us to go to Him. Without difficulty, many of us would never learn to pray. What is the best way to learn how to pray? Simply do it by speaking directly to God. He will guide us in our praying. In the same way, the Spirit helps us in our weakness. We do not know what we ought to pray for, but the Spirit himself intercedes for us with groans that words cannot express. And he who searches our hearts knows the mind of the Spirit, because the Spirit intercedes for the saints in accordance with God's will (Romans 8:26-27). The Spirit of God moves our spirit to pray. God assures us He will guide us.

Nearly all the commands to pray in the Bible are in the plural. That is, God commands we pray together; in the assembly of believers, in families, in small groups, with friends, and neighbors. Christians, the people of God, will seek out God at all times. When we pray together and for each other what will we need to do?

- Pray with faith.
  And without faith it is impossible to please God, because anyone who comes to him must believe that he exists and that he rewards those who earnestly seek him. (Hebrews 11:6)
- Pray with sensitivity.
  Pray with a heart that is led by the Holy Spirit.
- Thank God for others.
  I thank my God every time I remember you. (Philippians 1:3)
- Begin and end with worship.
  Don't rush into request but take time to worship God.
- Thank God.
  All asking without thanksgiving makes for sour Christians.
- Repent and forgive.
  Be sensitive of the need to repent or find forgiveness.
- Listen to others.
  When you pray together, stay on the same theme until everyone is finished praying. Learn to be comfortable with silence. Be sensitive to what God is saying.
- Speak up.
  It's difficult to pray with others if they cannot hear you.
- Pray in short sentences.
  Let others have opportunity to pray. Involve as many people as possible who are gathered to pray.
- Pray but don't gossip.
  We need to protect the privacy and dignity of those we pray for. When you pray together be careful not to cross the line from prayer request to gossip.
- Persevere in prayer.
  If you have prayed for items before, continue to do so. God will answer in His time. We are to persevere in our requests.
- Leave results to God.
  Praying to God does not obligate Him to act. It invites Him to act!

POINT TO PONDER

Our immediate response towards others is to pray.

VERSE TO REMEMBER

In the same way, the Spirit helps us in our weakness. We do not know what we ought to pray for, but the Spirit himself intercedes for us with groans that words cannot express.
(Romans 8:26)

QUESTION TO CONSIDER

Have you developed the habit of praying with others?

PRAYER FOCUS

Without praying to God, we would only be talking amongst ourselves.

DAY 28 JOURNAL

_____

_____

_____

_____

_____

_____

_____

_____

_____

_____

_____

_____

_____

_____

_____

_____

_____

Pray for Our Growth

Day 29

DEMONSTRATING GOD'S LORDSHIP

If you love me, you will obey what I command.
(John 14:15)

We grow by following the Master.

Praying believers make quantum leaps in being more like Jesus. We are called to follow Jesus — we are Christ-followers, or disciples. A disciple is a learner, imitator and one who espouses the values and practices of the Master. For believers, we have the added benefit of the Spirit of God to equip, encourage, remind, rebuke, convict and discipline — all to make us more like Jesus. The more we are in tune with the Master, the more we will be like Him.

Prayer is given to enhance our relationship to King Jesus. At the foundation of prayer is the understanding we are "minute men for God." We are constantly in attention to God's will and desires. Whatever He says goes. Wherever He tells me to go, I will go. Whatever He tells me to say, I will say. Without our response to Him, we really do not have obedience. Obedience shows how much we love God and control has been given to Him in our lives.

Those who obey God find Him to be joyful and not burdensome. This is love for God: to obey his commands. And his commands are not burdensome (1 John 5:3). However, if we decide to live independent of His will our lives will be a struggle — we may even find we are fighting against God (Acts 5:39).

Several of Jesus' disciples wanted to learn how to pray. They needed to be taught of the Master. Jesus taught them to pray in what we know now as the Lord's Prayer.

"This, then, is how you should pray: "Our Father in heaven, hallowed be your name, your kingdom come, your will be done on earth as it is in heaven. Give us today our daily bread. Forgive us our debts, as we also have forgiven our debtors. And lead us not into temptation, but deliver us from the evil one. For yours is the kingdom and the power and the glory forever. Amen'

(Matthew 6:9-13)

It was assumes that Christians would pray together. Although we cannot readily see this in English, all the pronouns in the Lord's Prayer are in plural. These were not words to be spoken individually but together, with agreement in the Spirit.

What can we see from the Lord's Prayer?

- Reverence
  Our Father in heaven, hallowed be your name. We begin with worship, giving Him glory and honor. Focus on who God is and His greatness.
- Response
  Your kingdom come, your will be done on earth as it is in heaven. In response to God's character, we give control over to the Holy Spirit. Surrender is important during this time. Include confession as well.
- Requests
  Give us today our daily bread. Forgive us our debts, as we also have forgiven our debtors. Since God already knows what we need even before we ask (Matthew 6:8) this is not so much to inform God as it is an affirmation of God's provision. A prayer journal is useful here. Record your requests for all prayer requests God brings to mind.
- Readiness
  And lead us not into temptation, but deliver us from the evil one. When we near the end of our prayer time, we want to be able to lead a life worthy of what God. We pray for readiness as we ready ourselves for daily living. We take spiritual warfare seriously. We prepare by checking again our willingness to let God direct our lives. Our battles are not fought with flesh or blood. It is of the Spirit — God needs to have complete control of our lives. Prayer, commitment, Scripture memory and meditation enhance God's presence in our lives.
- Reverence
  For yours is the kingdom and the power and the glory forever. Amen.' We conclude by praising Him and continued focus on who He is. We rest knowing God is in complete control.

The focus in this prayer is clearly God. He is first, last and everything in between. We come to Him for who He is. Our requests are important because they reflect our need. By bringing them to God, we acknowledge He is good enough and great enough to take care of every matter. When we grow in prayer we learn to follow God.

POINT TO PONDER

We grow by following the Master.

VERSE TO REMEMBER

If you love me, you will obey what I command.
(John 14:15)

QUESTION TO CONSIDER

Have you put into practice, Jesus' model for prayer?

PRAYER FOCUS

Take an accelerated step of growth by praying together.

DAY 29 JOURNAL

_____

_____

_____

_____

_____

_____

_____

_____

_____

_____

_____

_____

_____

_____

_____

_____

_____

Day 30

DEMONSTRATING GOD'S LOVE

> *For it is God who works in you to will and to act according to his good purpose.*
> (Philippians 2:13)

Love is a choice made through prayer.

If someone told you he loved you everyday yet never did anything to show how much he cared, you would begin to wonder if his word were true. After awhile, you question the words "I love you," said so casually, and wonder if it meant anything to the other person. Love demands action. In fact, our actions indicate what we love. If someone examined your life for several weeks, he would get an idea of what you really love; what is your passion in life. You can't help but demonstrate what you love and what drives you.

Love is more than mere words. The decision to love stems from the heart and reveals itself in concrete action. We love God in our hearts and it shows in how we live life. Words of love without actions beg the question whether that love is real. When the Spirit of God works within us our hearts change and we follow God. It's the heart change that makes it possible for life change. For it is God who works in you to will and to act according to his good purpose (Philippians 2:13).

Love always shows itself in action. As we follow Jesus, let's allow His example to be ours,

> *This is how we know what love is: Jesus Christ laid down his life for us. And we ought to lay down our lives for our brothers. If anyone has material possessions and sees his brother in need but has no pity on him, how can the love of God be in him? Dear children, let us not love with words or tongue but with actions and in truth.*
> (1 John 3:16-18)

When Jesus went to the cross, it was not a trivial decision. His prayers in the Garden of Gethsemane illustrated the deep struggle within Him. He even sweated drops of blood His prayers were so intense. And being in anguish, he prayed more earnestly, and his sweat was like drops of blood falling to the ground (Luke 22:44). The decision to go to the cross was born in prayer and confirmed in His heart.

In prayer, seemingly impossible complexities become clear. Difficult decisions are apparent. Even when we are called on to love those who hate us, our enemies, are possible when we go to God in prayer. In prayer, we are called upon to pray for our enemies. But I tell you: Love your enemies and pray for those who persecute you (Matthew 5:44). God changes us through His Spirit and great love. The Apostle Paul's prayed for believers to see the immense love of God and so love greatly as well.

> *I pray that out of his glorious riches he may strengthen you with power through his Spirit in your inner being, so that Christ may dwell in your hearts through faith. And I pray that you, being rooted and established in love, may have power, together with all the saints, to grasp how wide and long and high and deep is the love of Christ, and to know this love that surpasses knowledge — that you may be filled to the measure of all the fullness of God.*
>
> (Ephesians 3:16-19)

It's possible. Read that last line again. We can be so filled with God's love that the fullness of God dwells in us.

POINT TO PONDER

Love is a choice made through prayer.

VERSE TO REMEMBER

For it is God who works in you to will and to act according to his good purpose. (Philippians 2:13)

QUESTION TO CONSIDER

Does God control your life to the point that He can count on you to love others?

PRAYER FOCUS

Ask God to give you His love to love others.

DAY 30 JOURNAL

DEMONSTRATING GOD'S GRACE

> *As God's fellow workers we urge you not to receive God's grace in vain. For he says, "In the time of my favor I heard you, and in the day of salvation I helped you." I tell you, now is the time of God's favor, now is the day of salvation.*
>
> (2 Corinthians 6:1-2)

Those who receive God's favor must pass it on.

God's grace is His unmerited favor; that is, we did not earn it. He gives it to us freely. We grow when we pass God's favor to others. We who receive God's grace must repent of not demonstrating grace to others; of limiting our understanding of grace to salvation alone. We need fresh grace from the Lord to live out His heart.

We begin our spiritual journey when we pray to receive God's saving grace. At that moment, God forgives us of all wrong we have done and will do. Jesus paid the price on the cross when we call to God; we receive the forgiveness of sin and a new life.

As a new person in Christ, each day is a grace adventure. We grow in our knowledge and experience of God's goodness. But grow in the grace and knowledge of our Lord and Savior Jesus Christ (2 Peter 3:18). The more we know God, the more we live by His grace. The sweetness of God is so good; we begin treating others the same way.

> *The end of all things is near. Therefore be clear minded and self-controlled so that you can pray. Above all, love each other deeply, because love covers over a multitude of sins. Offer hospitality to one another without grumbling. Each one should use whatever gift he has received to serve others, faithfully administering God's grace in its various forms. If anyone speaks, he should do it as one speaking the very words of God. If anyone serves, he should do it with the strength God provides, so that in all things God may be praised through Jesus Christ. To him be the glory and the power for ever and ever. Amen.*
>
> (1 Peter 4:7-11)

We grow when we pray together and thank God for His grace. We discover when God controls our lives He showers us with even more grace.

> All the believers were one in heart and mind. No one claimed that any of his possessions
> was his own, but they shared everything they had. With great power the apostles continued
> to testify to the resurrection of the Lord Jesus, and much grace was upon them all.
>
> (Acts 4:32-33)

We won't lack grace as long as we follow God. The temptation of pride
is constant when God is working in our lives. When we do it God's way and
humble ourselves, he provides extra grace. But he gives us more grace. That
is why Scripture says: "God opposes the proud but gives grace to the humble"
(James 4:6).

How can we grow in grace?

· Pray together
   *Pray for us. We are sure that we have a clear conscience and desire to live honorably in
   every way.* (Hebrews 13:18)
   Trust God

   From persecution came the growth and expansion of the early church!
   *Now those who had been scattered by the persecution in connection with Stephen traveled
   as far as Phoenicia, Cyprus and Antioch, telling the message only to Jews. Some of them,
   however, men from Cyprus and Cyrene, went to Antioch and began to speak to Greeks
   also, telling them the good news about the Lord Jesus. The Lord's hand was with them, and
   a great number of people believed and turned to the Lord. News of this reached the ears of
   the church at Jerusalem, and they sent Barnabas to Antioch. When he arrived and saw
   the evidence of the grace of God, he was glad and encouraged them all to remain true to
   the Lord with all their hearts. He was a good man, full of the Holy Spirit and faith, and a
   great number of people were brought to the Lord.* (Acts 11:19-24)
· Practice grace

   Be gracious in your actions, attitudes and speech.

POINT TO PONDER

Those who receive God's favor must pass it on.

VERSE TO REMEMBER

But grow in the grace and knowledge of our Lord and Savior Jesus Christ.
(2 Peter 3:18)

QUESTION TO CONSIDER

Do you become more gracious as God gives you more grace?

PRAYER FOCUS

God, I was saved by grace; now help me live by grace.

DAY 31 JOURNAL

_____

_____

_____

_____

_____

_____

_____

_____

_____

_____

_____

_____

_____

_____

_____

_____

_____

_____

_____

_____

_____

_____

_____

Day 32

DEMONSTRATING GOD'S MERCY

Shouldn't you have had mercy on your fellow servant just as I had on you?
(Matthew 18:33)

Mercy demonstrates strength mixed with love.

We live in an age that believes each person deserves what they get. It sounds right but it is not. Much of what we receive is by grace, getting what we do not deserve and also mercy, not receiving what we should get. Mercy is not weakness or giving in. Mercy is part of God's justice system; it demonstrates the compassionate heart of God. "This is what the LORD Almighty says: 'Administer true justice; show mercy and compassion to one another (Zechariah 7:9).

Prayer allows us to get in touch with God and His heart for others. We learn we don't treat people as they deserve but as God would treat them. We learn it is not working harder that pleases God but being right with God! For I desire mercy, not sacrifice, and acknowledgment of God rather than burnt offerings (Hosea 6:6). If God were to treat us as we deserve, we would be consumed in a moment. Because of the Lord's great love we are not consumed, for his compassions never fail. They are new every morning; great is your faithfulness. (Lamentations 3:22-23)

When we fail to show mercy, we fail to demonstrate the compassion of God. It's when we are merciful that the character of God shines forth. When we are merciful God also blesses us. Blessed are the merciful, for they will be shown mercy (Matthew 5:7).

How then do we obtain a heart of mercy?

- Remember how much you have been forgiven by God
  Who is a God like you, who pardons sin and forgives the transgression of the remnant of his inheritance? You do not stay angry forever but delight to show mercy. (Micah 7:18)
- Remember how much others are in need of forgiveness
  We all, like sheep, have gone astray, each of us has turned to his own way; and the LORD

has laid on him the iniquity of us all. (Isaiah 53:6)

· Remember we all still deal with sin
When they kept on questioning him, he straightened up and said to them, "If any one of you is without sin, let him be the first to throw a stone at her." (John 8:7)

· Remember God's offer for forgiveness is still valid
All the prophets testify about him that everyone who believes in him receives forgiveness of sins through his name." (Acts 10:43)

· Remember God's mercy is greater than our mercy
What then shall we say? Is God unjust? Not at all! For he says to Moses, "I will have mercy on whom I have mercy, and I will have compassion on whom I have compassion." It does not, therefore, depend on man's desire or effort, but on God's mercy. (Romans 9:14-16)

When we pray and align our hearts with God, we will discover His mercy is immense and will prevent us from playing the role of the judge or avenger. God will have His time to administer His justice. Do not take revenge, my friends, but leave room for God's wrath, for it is written: "It is mine to avenge; I will repay," says the Lord (Romans 12:19). In the meantime, we are to demonstrate God's mercy.

POINT TO PONDER

Mercy demonstrates strength mixed with love.

VERSE TO REMEMBER

Blessed are the merciful, for they will be shown mercy.
(Matthew 5:7)

QUESTION TO CONSIDER

Do you easily grant mercy?

PRAYER FOCUS

O God, may your mercy flow through me.

DAY 32 JOURNAL

Day 33

DEMONSTRATING GOD'S TRUTH

> *These are the things you are to do: Speak the truth to each other, and render true and sound judgment in your courts; do not plot evil against your neighbor, and do not love to swear falsely. I hate all this," declares the Lord.*
> (Zechariah 8:16-17)

The truth will set you free.

Truth has gotten a bad rap in recent days. White lies, bending the truth, exaggerations, and little fibs seem to be all the rage. Little by little, our souls weaken when truth is not upheld. We need to uphold truth for it is the way to freedom. To the Jews who had believed him, Jesus said, "If you hold to my teaching, you are really my disciples. Then you will know the truth, and the truth will set you free" (John 8:31-32). The truth of God leads to purity of soul. Sanctify them by the truth; your word is truth (John 17:17).

Jesus warned of a day when sound teaching will not be tolerated. For the time will come when men will not put up with sound doctrine. Instead, to suit their own desires, they will gather around them a great number of teachers to say what their itching ears want to hear (2 Timothy 4:3). Strange isn't it. We prize revelation from God but want to selectively pick and choose what God will say.

The Bible is God's truth, the sword of the Spirit. Take the helmet of salvation and the sword of the Spirit, which is the word of God (Ephesians 6:17). The Word of God is a revealer of the heart and soul. For the word of God is living and active. Sharper than any double-edged sword, it penetrates even to dividing soul and spirit, joints and marrow; it judges the thoughts and attitudes of the heart (Hebrews 4:12). Without the Bible, the word of God, we won't have a weapon. We need to know our Bible and skillfully wield it.

Since the Word of God is such a powerful weapon, it must be used with extreme care. Yielding it carelessly can wound or even kill. The truth of God needs to be balanced with the love of God. Instead, speaking the truth in love, we will in all things grow up into him who is the Head, that is, Christ

(Ephesians 4:15). In God, truth and love is inseparable. True worshipers need to come to God with both. Yet a time is coming and has now come when the true worshipers will worship the Father in spirit and truth, for they are the kind of worshipers the Father seeks (John 4:23).

Our lives then need to be lived in truth and with love.

- How much of God's word do you have in you?
  The old adage that you only have as much of the Bible as you have within you. If all Bibles were removed, how much of it would you retain within you
- How much of the Bible have you read?
  Without the Bible, our only offensive weapon, we would be like unarmed soldiers for God.
- Have a plan to read the Bible
  Whether you are reading the Bible in a year or other amounts, plan or you plan to fail.
- How do you plan to put it into practice?
  The Bible is primarily about transformation and not for information.
- Blend truth with love
  Truth without love is dry, heartless, and cold. Love without truth is sentimental, syrupy, mushy and unsound. Only when truth is blended with love do we have a sense of what God is all about.
- Pray Scripture to incorporate head and heart.
  Prayer is the great mixer that buries truth deep within our hearts where it simmers with God's Spirit to bring about a pleasing aroma.

Listen to the Psalmist as he recounts his encounter with truth and how he was set free.

Come and listen, all you who fear God; let me tell you what he has done for me.
I cried out to him with my mouth; his praise was on my tongue. If I had cherished sin in my heart,
the Lord would not have listened; but God has surely listened and heard my voice in prayer.
Praise be to God, who has not rejected my prayer or withheld his love from me!

(Psalm 66:16-20)

It's true for King David then it is also true for us as well.

POINT TO PONDER

The truth will set you free.

VERSE TO REMEMBER

To the Jews who had believed him, Jesus said, "If you hold to my teaching, you are really my disciples. Then you will know the truth, and the truth will set you free."
(John 8:31-32)

QUESTION TO CONSIDER

How much of the truth of God do you carry within you?

PRAYER FOCUS

Take in truth and mix with love to form a soul set free.

DAY 33 JOURNAL

Day 34

DEMONSTRATING GOD'S LIFE IN THE SPIRIT

---

*Therefore, brothers, we have an obligation — but it is not to the sinful nature,
to live according to it. For if you live according to the sinful nature, you will die; but if
by the Spirit you put to death the misdeeds of the body, you will live, because those
who are led by the Spirit of God are sons of God.*
(Romans 8:12-14)

Victory in the Spirit demands the defeat of the flesh.

We are involved in a spiritual war that demands spiritual weapons. We have
the Devil, the flesh and the world, with its system that is contrary to the way
of God. For everything in the world - the cravings of sinful man, the lust of his
eyes and the boasting of what he has and does - comes not from the Father but
from the world (1 John 2:16). The flesh, the remnants of our sinful nature war
against the things of the spirit. Victory depends on the Spirit controlling our
lives and putting down or the defeat of the flesh on a daily basis. We can't have
both. I know that nothing good lives in me, that is, in my sinful nature. For I
have the desire to do what is good, but I cannot carry it out (Romans 7:18).
When the sinful nature or the flesh is in control of our lives, the Spirit of God is
not allowed to operate. In the same way, when the Spirit is in control, the flesh
is neutralized.

The Spirit of God reigns in our lives to the extent we allow Him. When
we act in the flesh, the Spirit of God stands aside. The Apostle Paul recognized
when he was acting in the flesh and when he operated in the power of the Holy
Spirit. True spiritual life and vitality come when God reigns in us. The spiritual
war we are involved with means we have to fight within the spiritual realm.

Be assured Jesus has won the victory! We fight from victory, claiming what
has already been won.

· Prepare for spiritual battle
*Finally, be strong in the Lord and in his mighty power. Put on the full armor of God so
that you can take your stand against the devil's schemes. For our struggle is not against
flesh and blood, but against the rulers, against the authorities, against the powers of this*

dark world and against the spiritual forces of evil in the heavenly realms.
(Ephesians 6:10-12)

· Set your mind on things above
The mind of sinful man is death, but the mind controlled by the Spirit is life and peace.
(Romans 8:6)

· Don't compromise with sin
Therefore, since Christ suffered in his body, arm yourselves also with the same attitude, because he who has suffered in his body is done with sin. (1 Peter 4:1)

· Don't rely on the flesh
For it is we who are the circumcision, we who worship by the Spirit of God, who glory in Christ Jesus, and who put no confidence in the flesh. (Philippians 3:3)

· Stay alert
"Watch and pray so that you will not fall into temptation. The spirit is willing, but the body is weak." (Matthew 26:41)

· Know and use your sword
For the word of God is living and active. Sharper than any double-edged sword, it penetrates even to dividing soul and spirit, joints and marrow; it judges the thoughts and attitudes of the heart. (Hebrews 4:12)

· Pray constantly
And pray in the Spirit on all occasions with all kinds of prayers and requests. With this in mind, be alert and always keep on praying for all the saints. (Ephesians 6:18)

In your inner being, the new creation, you desire to follow God with all your heart. I desire to do your will, O my God; your law is within my heart (Psalm 40:8). Nurture that aspect of your life by centering on God.

POINT TO PONDER

Victory in the Spirit demands the defeat of the flesh.

VERSE TO REMEMBER

For if you live according to the sinful nature, you will die; but if by the Spirit you put to death the misdeeds of the body, you will live.
(Romans 8:13)

QUESTION TO CONSIDER

Who will rule in your life today; the Spirit or the flesh?

PRAYER FOCUS

Nourishing the Spirit and starving the flesh makes for a healthy Christian.

DAY 34 JOURNAL

_____

_____

_____

_____

_____

_____

_____

_____

_____

_____

_____

_____

_____

_____

_____

_____

_____

_____

_____

_____

_____

_____

_____

_____

_____

Day 35

DEMONSTRATING CHRIST'S SERVANTHOOD

> *Jesus called them together and said, "You know that the rulers of the Gentiles lord it over them, and their high officials exercise authority over them. Not so with you. Instead, whoever wants to become great among you must be your servant, and whoever wants to be first must be your slave — just as the Son of Man did not come to be served, but to serve, and to give his life as a ransom for many."*
> (Matthew 20:25-28)

We serve others best when we first serve God.

At the moment of salvation we became children of God. By our new nature, we are his and desire to serve God. It's not just for the elite but for everyone. He gifted each believer with talents, time and treasure to serve Him. When we serve others with the power of God for the Name of God, He is honored. It's actually quite freeing knowing all we have is from God. He won't ask us to do what He has not equipped us to do. But he will do in and through us the impossible!

Our prayer life, communication with God, leads to sensitivity towards others. He has people all around you He would like you to serve today. The quality of your service will depend on your preparation of heart before serving. Have you ever walked into a restaurant and you knew the waitress or waiter is having a bad day? They don't have to tell you, you just know it. Now, they will take your order and bring out your food. In that moment, you could give a word of encouragement, a large tim or invite them to share what is on their mind. You simply make yourself available for God's working.

When you pray to God and tell him of your availability, you place yourself in a posture to serve. You want the fragrance of Christ to surround your service and bless others. Now this is a moment by moment decision you can make. Will God be the Lord of your life for the next 5 seconds? Eventually, you will rely on God as a way of life. How do you learn to serve with the Spirit of God empowering you? How do you serve God and others with a great attitude?

· Learn from Jesus

Now that I, your Lord and Teacher, have washed your feet, you also should wash one another's feet. (John 13:14)

If the King of Kings stooped down to serve, we have no excuse not to serve others.

- Seek to please God

I tell you the truth, no servant is greater than his master, nor is a messenger greater than the one who sent him. Now that you know these things, you will be blessed if you do them. (John 13:16-17)

The joy of our live should be to please God. Pleasing God needs to be our life's desire. The more we know what God loves and hates, the better we can please Him.

- Humility

Your attitude should be the same as that of Christ Jesus: Who, being in very nature God, did not consider equality with God something to be grasped, but made himself nothing, taking the very nature of a servant, being made in human likeness. And being found in appearance as a man, he humbled himself and became obedient to death—even death on a cross! (Philippians 2:5-8)

Jesus was not proud but humble. His humility made Him the Supreme Servant.

- Obedience

Jesus gave them this answer: "I tell you the truth, the Son can do nothing by himself; he can do only what he sees his Father doing, because whatever the Father does the Son also does. For the Father loves the Son and shows him all he does. (John 5:19-20)

The proof is in the pudding. When we put into practice what we know God wants us to do, that's called obedience. God's not looking for our opinion. He's looking whether we will actually follow Him.

POINT TO PONDER

We serve others best when we first serve God.

VERSE TO REMEMBER

Sitting down, Jesus called the Twelve and said, "If anyone wants to be first, he must be the very last, and the servant of all."
(Mark 9:35)

QUESTION TO CONSIDER

If God were to give you a mid-life report, would He say you served Him with "5-star" service?

PRAYER FOCUS

God, help me serve others with sensitivity and joy.

DAY 35 JOURNAL

_____

_____

_____

_____

_____

_____

_____

_____

_____

_____

_____

_____

_____

_____

_____

_____

_____

_____

_____

_____

_____

Pray for Other Believers

Day 36

PRAYING FOR WISDOM

> *If any of you lacks wisdom, he should ask God, who gives generously to all without finding fault, and it will be given to him.*
>
> (James 1:5)

The wisest thing you can do is to ask God.

When praying by yourself or with others, the most essential issue is to approach God. When we do, He invites us to ask for wisdom. Wisdom is not only knowledge but the skill to use knowledge God has given us in a particular situation. You may be facing key decisions in the near future. You need God's wisdom. Others may need wisdom about a relationship. What are they to do? Pray for God's wisdom. In James 1:5, God promises He will give wisdom to us generously if we will only ask Him.

In prayer, the pressure is off us to come up with answers. God is the One holding all the answers. God is eager to give us wisdom and give us more understanding if only we would ask. The Apostle Paul prayed for the Ephesians, I pray also that the eyes of your heart may be enlightened in order that you may know the hope to which he has called you, the riches of his glorious inheritance in the saints (Ephesians 1:18). He prayed that these believers would know just how great their hope is in Jesus Christ; how much God had in store for them. He prayed that when they realized glory, they would change. They would no longer complain, be dissatisfied, compare, frown, etc. He wanted God to give them wisdom to see their true, rich position in Christ.

King Solomon could have asked for many things but the one thing he asked God was wisdom. In Proverbs he instructs others to do the same.

My son, if you accept my words and store up my commands within you, turning your ear to wisdom and applying your heart to understanding, and if you call out for insight and cry aloud for understanding, and if you look for it as for silver and search for it as for hidden treasure, then you will understand the fear of the Lord and find the knowledge of God. For the Lord gives wisdom, and from his mouth come knowledge and understanding. (Proverbs 2:1-6)

King David prayed that he would receive God's wisdom so that he would live a life pleasing to God.

> Teach me, O LORD, to follow your decrees; then I will keep them to the end. Give me understanding, and I will keep your law and obey it with all my heart. Direct me in the path of your commands, for there I find delight. Turn my heart toward your statutes and not toward selfish gain. Turn my eyes away from worthless things; preserve my life according to your word. Fulfill your promise to your servant, so that you may be feared. Take away the disgrace I dread, for your laws are good. How I long for your precepts! Preserve my life in your righteousness.
> (Psalm 119:33-40)

David prayed for wisdom so that in practical ways, his life would honor God. The most practical request we can make is when we ask God for wisdom, provided we intend to obey what He says.

When God grants us wisdom it goes deep within our soul. Surely you desire truth in the inner parts; you teach me wisdom in the inmost place (Psalm 51:6). God is not only looking for proper behavior but a changed heart that determines the actions in our lives. Who is wise and understanding among you? Let him show it by his good life, by deeds done in the humility that comes from wisdom. But the wisdom that comes from heaven is first of all pure; then peace-loving, considerate, submissive, full of mercy and good fruit, impartial and sincere. (James 3:13, 17)

Wisdom also helps us to prioritize our lives. Time is too short not to live it strategically and with purpose. Teach us to number our days aright, that we may gain a heart of wisdom (Psalm 90:12).

POINT TO PONDER

The wisest thing you can do is to ask God.

VERSE TO REMEMBER

If any of you lacks wisdom, he should ask God, who gives generously to all without finding fault, and it will be given to him.
(James 1:5)

QUESTION TO CONSIDER

Do you pray before you act or do you act and then pray?

PRAYER FOCUS

Only You God hold true wisdom. Show me what I need to know.

DAY 36 JOURNAL

_____

_____

_____

_____

_____

_____

_____

_____

_____

_____

_____

_____

_____

_____

_____

_____

_____

_____

_____

_____

_____

_____

Day 37

PRAYING FOR STRENGTH

> *But my brothers who went up with me made the hearts of the people melt with fear. I,*
> *however, followed the Lord my God wholeheartedly. So on that day Moses swore to me,*
> *'The land on which your feet have walked will be your inheritance and that of your*
> *children forever, because you have followed the Lord my God wholeheartedly.*
> (Joshua 14:8-9)

God will empower you to do what He has called you to do.

Significant contributions from saints of the past happened because they relied on God's strength. Difficulties surrounded them. Never was the situation ideal. Always confrontation met them as they followed God's will. It was not a matter of trying harder but God empowering them to finish the task.

Think of the seeming impossibilities that stood before Moses as he led the Israelites out of Egypt. The naysayers were all around discouraging him from continuing. Yet, God worked through all difficulties. He empowered Moses, by performing miraculous signs, hardening then softening the heart of pharaoh, and parted then closed the Red Sea to rid themselves of the Egyptians.

The early church had quite a challenge. Jesus told them to spread the gospel to the known world. The believers numbering only about 500 at the time of Christ's crucifixion would have seemed incapable of such a great task. Yet, God's worked through all difficulties again. In a few short weeks, the Spirit of God came in full power and in a single day, three thousand came to the Lord. In only three centuries, Christianity gained recognition as the official religion under Constantine. Christianity had conquered the Roman Empire!

Seeming impossibilities will be accomplished when we seek God for His empowering.

> *He gives strength to the weary and increases the power of the weak. Even youths*
> *grow tired and weary, and young men stumble and fall; but those who hope in the LORD*
> *will renew their strength. They will soar on wings like eagles; they will run and*
> *not grow weary, they will walk and not be faint.*
> (Isaiah 40:29-31)

God provides supernatural strength to continue when natural strength gives out.

The more we desire to do God's will, the more we will need to pray for his strength and empowering. As long as we know God has an assignment for us, He will give us strength. I can do everything through him who gives me strength (Philippians 4:13). Habakkuk writes of God's supernatural strength because the Lord Himself is his strength. The Sovereign LORD is my strength; he makes my feet like the feet of a deer, he enables me to go on the heights. (Habakkuk 3:19).

As you pray for others and yourself, God will give spiritual and physical strength for all you will face. Speaking to the Church of Philadelphia, Jesus says, I know your deeds. See, I have placed before you an open door that no one can shut. I know that you have little strength, yet you have kept my word and have not denied my name (Revelation 3:8). God tells us what to do, He provides a way, and He will provide us strength.

POINT TO PONDER

God will empower you to do what He has called you to do.

VERSE TO REMEMBER

The Sovereign LORD is my strength; he makes my feet like the feet of a deer, he enables me to go on the heights.
(Habakkuk 3:19)

QUESTION TO CONSIDER

Who will you pray for that is in need of God's strength?

PRAYER FOCUS

Our strength is limited but God's has no limit.

DAY 37 JOURNAL

Day 38

PRAYING FOR HEALING

> Is any one of you in trouble? He should pray. Is anyone happy? Let him sing songs of praise.
> Is any one of you sick? He should call the elders of the church to pray over him and anoint him
> with oil in the name of the Lord. And the prayer offered in faith will make the sick person well;
> the Lord will raise him up. If he has sinned, he will be forgiven. Therefore confess your sins
> to each other and pray for each other so that you may be healed. The prayer of a
> righteous man is powerful and effective.
>
> (James 5:13-17)

God is Our Great Physician

When someone is sick, God tells us to gather together and pray. Whether the sickness is physical, emotional, or spiritual, God instructs us to pray. As the church gathers to call upon God, the church gathers to pray on behalf of the sick. In James 5, the situation is spiritual sickness. The person is need of salvation. The elders are gathered and so is the church. Confession takes place leading to forgiveness of sin. The key is the prayer of a righteous man or men for the sick. God honors the prayers of the godly.

When there is a need for physical healing, the pattern is the same. God desires that we all come to health; with ultimate healing coming when we receive a new incorruptible body. It's important to note that God still decides how He will answer prayer. It's His will, His plan, and His timing. He may answer "yes" and provide immediate healing, He may answer "wait" or He may answer "no." When God does not heal, it may be His purpose to glory Himself through our weaknesses.

Jesus had large crowds of people come to Him and He healed them. When the sun was setting, the people brought to Jesus all who had various kinds of sickness, and laying his hands on each one, he healed them (Luke 4:40). His ultimate healing, for our souls, came when Jesus died on the cross, making it possible for our spiritually dead condition to receive life. He himself bore our sins in his body on the tree, so that we might die to sins and live for righteousness; by his wounds you have been healed (1 Peter 2:24).

Praying for the sick may also include casting out of demons. They drove out many demons and anointed many sick people with oil and healed them (Mark 6:13). It's a spiritual issue. A hardened heart is not acceptable to God and may is a deterrent to healing. For this people's heart has become calloused; they hardly hear with their ears, and they have closed their eyes. Otherwise they might see with their eyes, hear with their ears, understand with their hearts and turn, and I would heal them (Acts 28:27).

God is sovereign and will do what He wills. Yet, He calls us to pray to Him and call others to join us. It is our responsibility to pray to God for the sick. We need to bring others before the throne of grace. God sometimes answers "yes," sometimes He answers "no" and sometimes He answers "wait."

POINT TO PONDER

God is Our Great Physician.

VERSE TO REMEMBER

Jesus said to him, "Receive your sight; your faith has healed you."
(Luke 18:42)

QUESTION TO CONSIDER

Have you sought the Great Physician for healing?

PRAYER FOCUS

Healing the whole person is God's ultimate goal.

DAY 38 JOURNAL

Day 39

PRAYING FOR WORKERS

> *He told them, "The harvest is plentiful, but the workers are few. Ask the Lord of the harvest,*
> *therefore, to send out workers into his harvest field.*
> (Luke 10:2)

More workers for God begin with prayer.

Jesus needed more workers and found disciples. The church today needs
more workers also. Jesus prayed a long while before he chose the twelve. We
need to enter into a time of prayer for the workers of the harvest. The church
was born out of a prayer meeting. The early church was found praying and God
answered with power as the Holy Spirit came. But you will receive power when
the Holy Spirit comes on you; and you will be my witnesses in Jerusalem, and in
all Judea and Samaria, and to the ends of the earth (Acts 1:8). We need to pray
for workers who are in the harvest field now and for future workers.

Prayer is so vital in our evangelistic endeavors that witnessing without
praying is like going parachuting without a parachute. The Prophet Samuel, in
speaking to the people about following their new king thought it a great sin if
he failed to pray for the people. As for me, far be it from me that I should sin
against the Lord by failing to pray for you. And I will teach you the way that is
good and right. But be sure to fear the Lord and serve him faithfully with all
your heart; consider what great things he has done for you (1 Samuel 12:23-24).
We need to prepare the harvest field with constant praying.

The Apostle Paul was so aware of the spiritual nature of what he was doing
that he asked people to pray always given the opportunity. He did not want to
take for granted that the Holy Spirit was active and powerful in His life. He
never wanted to get to the place where he would minister without God; he
didn't want to take God lightly.

> *And pray in the Spirit on all occasions with all kinds of prayers and requests.*
> *With this in mind, be alert and always keep on praying for all the saints. Pray also for me,*
> *that whenever I open my mouth, words may be given me so that I will fearlessly*
> *make known the mystery of the gospel, for which I am an ambassador in chains.*

Pray that I may declare it fearlessly, as I should.
(Ephesians 6:18-20)

Pray for those who are in the work today. They could be local workers serving in the church, or at a para-church organization. Better yet, it is every believer that takes their identity in Christ seriously and is involved in the work of God. Pray that as a church and as people of God we all arrive at that point.

When Jesus told the disciples to pray that God would send workers into the harvest field, several things happened:

- The disciples began to pray about the harvest.
- The disciples began to have a burden about the harvest field.
- The disciples began to minister in the harvest field.
- The disciples were the answer to their own prayers!

How does one get a burden for the mission field? Many think you have to have an extraordinary experience with God to be involved in His work. It simply isn't so. You and I, as we pray about God's harvest field, God will give us a burden for the lost and use us in His work. It begins with prayer.

The world situation can be chaotic. They were during the first century. St. Peter had this admonition for the early believers, The end of all things is near. Therefore be clear minded and self-controlled so that you can pray (1 Peter 4:7). Many in the early church fully believed Jesus would return in their lifetime. They felt they had to do something. Old impulsive Peter, now the seasoned saint, calmed them down so they could seek God and pray. Their prayers transformed their hearts that led to turning the Roman Empire upside down as Christianity exploded across the land.

In missions, they speak of the ones that stay and the ones that go. Each has a part to do. Those that stay are encouraged to support the ones that go. The ones that go are encouraged to spread the gospel boldly. The key, whether one stays or goes, is to pray to the Lord that he will be involved in sending out workers into the harvest field.

POINT TO PONDER

More workers for God begin with prayer.

VERSE TO REMEMBER

He told them, "The harvest is plentiful, but the workers are few. Ask the Lord of the harvest, therefore, to send out workers into his harvest field.
(Luke 10:2)

QUESTION TO CONSIDER

Whether you are a sender or a goer, are you a pray-er?

PRAYER FOCUS

I pray for those who labor for you. I pray also for more workers.

DAY 39 JOURNAL

_____

_____

_____

_____

_____

_____

_____

_____

_____

_____

_____

_____

_____

_____

_____

_____

_____

_____

_____

_____

_____

_____

Day 40

PRAYING FOR THOSE IN AUTHORITY

> *I urge, then, first of all, that requests, prayers, intercession and thanksgiving be made for everyone — for kings and all those in authority, that we may live peaceful and quiet lives in all godliness and holiness.*
>
> (1 Timothy 2:1-2)

Everyone in authority needs prayer.

We need to pray for our leaders. Whether it is the President of the United States, senators, congressmen, police chiefs, leader of the Girl Scout troop, or president of our home owners association, they all need prayer. God instituted government, authority and leaders. Even when leaders are evil, He still would have us honor their position.

Notice when the Spirit of God withdrew from King Saul. He hotly pursued David out of jealousy. Several times David had opportunity to take Saul's life. Yet, he did not because Saul was anointed of God. The LORD rewards every man for his righteousness and faithfulness. The LORD delivered you into my hands today, but I would not lay a hand on the LORD's anointed (1 Samuel 26:23).

When the Apostle Paul instructed believers, living in a time when Christians were brutalized and murdered, he still urged them to obey and pray for the authorities of the day. Everyone must submit himself to the governing authorities, for there is no authority except that which God has established. The authorities that exist have been established by God (Romans 13:1). Notice his reasoning. It was not because they were just. It was because authority "has been established by God." Paul reasoned that it was God's business whom he allowed to rule and if God wanted to dispose of the ruler, then that was God's prerogative. In them meantime, we are to pray for God to work.

Praying and obeying authorities helped in their understanding of being sent. As God sent Jesus; He now sent them into the world, by His authority. When Jesus had called the Twelve together, he gave them power and authority to drive out all demons and to cure diseases, and he sent them out to preach the kingdom of God and to heal the sick (Luke 9:1-2). People who do not recognize authority quickly slide into rebellion, the reason why Lucifer fell.

When we submit to authority, we recognize the spiritual covering over us. Leaders are accountable to God and we benefit from their spiritual oversight. Obey your leaders and submit to their authority. They keep watch over you as men who must give an account. Obey them so that their work will be a joy, not a burden, for that would be of no advantage to you (Hebrews 13:17). Our prayers for leaders work both ways. Prayer invites God to assist our leaders do a better job. As a result of their service, we benefit because of their just rule and godly service.

When we pray to God on behalf of godly leaders, He grants our requests and they edify His people. Then I will give you shepherds after my own heart, who will lead you with knowledge and understanding (Jeremiah 3:15). Ultimately, we want leaders to be just and godly even if it may seem harsh to us. This is why I write these things when I am absent, that when I come I may not have to be harsh in my use of authority—the authority the Lord gave me for building you up, not for tearing you down. (2 Corinthians 13:10)

When you pray for those in authority, God hears. Ultimately, if we are not submissive to earthly authority, how will we ever learn to submit to heavenly authority?

POINT TO PONDER

Everyone in authority needs prayer.

VERSE TO REMEMBER

Obey your leaders and submit to their authority. They keep watch over you as men who must give an account. Obey them so that their work will be a joy, not a burden, for that would be of no advantage to you.
(Hebrews 13:17)

QUESTION TO CONSIDER

Do you pray more than you complain about your leaders?

PRAYER FOCUS

Lift up your leaders; don't tear them down.

DAY 40 JOURNAL